CREATIVE ACTION METHODS
IN GROUPWORK

"Miracles happen when there is a dedication to change oneself"
Farouk Kadoomi

CREATIVE ACTION METHODS
IN GROUPWORK

Andy Hickson

616.
891523
HIC

Speechmark Publishing Ltd
Telford Road • Bicester • Oxon OX26 4LQ • UK

- 3 JUL 2008

Published by
Speechmark Publishing Ltd, Telford Road, Bicester, Oxon OX26 4LQ
United Kingdom
www.speechmark.net

© Andy Hickson, 1995
Reprinted 1997, 2002, 2005

All rights reserved. The whole of this work including all text and illustrations is protected by copyright. No part of it may be copied, altered, adopted or otherwise exploited in any way without express prior permission, unless in accordance with the provisions of the Copyright Designs and Patents Act 1988 or in order to photocopy or make duplicating masters of those pages so indicated, without alteration and including copyright notices, for the express purposes of instruction and examination. No parts of this work may be otherwise be loaded, stored, manipulated, reproduced, or transmitted in any form or by any means, electronic or mechanical, including photocopying and recording or by any information, storage and retrieval system without prior permission from the publisher, on behalf of the copyright owner.

002-2278/Printed in Great Britain/1010

British Library Cataloguing in Publication Data
Hickson, Andy
Creative action methods in groupwork
   1. Psychodrama
   I. Title
   616.8'91523

ISBN 0 86388 407 5
(Previously published by Winslow Press Ltd under ISBN 0 86388 141 6)

CONTENTS

Foreword		vii
Acknowledgements		ix
Introduction		x
SECTION 1	Different Approaches to Action Methods	1
	Drama games	3
	Psychodrama	4
	Dramatherapy	7
	Theatre of the oppressed	9
	Ritual	13
SECTION 2	Methods and Techniques (Action in Action)	15
	Introduction	17
	The body in action	17
	The voice in action	41
	The senses in action	53
	Games in action	95
	Images in action	141
	Scenes in action	155
	Follow-up action	178
APPENDIX	*Associated therapies*	187
	Evaluation	190
	Bibliography	193
	Alphabetical list of activities	195

ANDY HICKSON is a theatre director, actor, playwright and group leader. He has toured all over the UK and performed plays and workshops for schools and community centres as well as social services, prisons, hospitals and theatres. He specializes in working with creative action methods and theatre of the oppressed techniques for actors, probation officers, teachers and therapists. He has recently run specialist workshops for: Inner London Probation Service, SOAS (University of London), Blackburn Youth Service, Institute of Dramatherapy (IDT) UK, IDT Norway, Royal London Hospital, The London Actors Invisible Theatre Group, British Telecom plc, Thames Water and Silent Scream – tackling bullying in schools. He is a founder member of Hey! Hey! Theatre Co Ltd, Twin Angles, Tie Tours and Scaley Ink Co.

FOREWORD

The decade of the 1960s has often, in hindsight, attracted harsh critical attention, focused upon illusory hopes of revolution and spurious images of freedom, which failed to be realized in the time which reasonable people allotted to them. What is often missed is the positive, liberating ideas that came out of the decade, which radically changed traditional ways of thinking and which are still with us in embattled forms. In many fields of human need, activity and endeavour, stress was taken away from the word and placed on action. By bringing the body into the equation, the complementary interaction of brain and body with the adding of emotion to thought and of the subconscious to the conscious will, the measure of the human being began to involve a totality of the personal processes and resources which could be developed and utilized to overcome the blocks, barriers and hazards which life presents to us. The escape from nineteenth-century prescriptive and proscriptive rationalism, and all the hang-ups it has engendered, lay in the gestalt and in group relationships and action. In this lay the real hope of freedom.

This freedom has been under heavy attack for some time now. The new emphasis on conformity and testing in schools is eroding all sense of learning by doing pleasurably and is reducing education to a list of quantifiable entities. We have been told that there is no such thing as society, only individuals, and in a rapidly changing world, in which the maximum amount of flexibility is needed to seize any opportunity, individuals are being educated to know and maintain their station in life. Rejecting even the materialist views of enlightenment which underlay nineteenth-century rationalist education, we seem to be moving to a situation of passive acceptance, where everyone is responsible for their own destinies and yet are totally unable to affect any single circumstance of their lives.

Brecht taught us that all learning should be pleasurable. Augusto Boal, drawing on the ideas and work of Paolo Freire, has shown very dramatically that the road to social revolution does not lie in pious political exhortation and easy solutions, but in group participation in painstaking and detailed re-examination of the veiled, but concrete, processes of exploitation and oppression. If recent events seem to have removed political revolution from the agenda for the foreseeable future and to have created, world-wide, a political nightmare in which neighbour is set against neighbour in bloody conflict, replete with atrocities, then whatever progress we can make towards a humane, peaceful and secure world for our children must, of necessity, begin with people meeting to work out their conflicts and establish a basis for harmonious co-operation. Andy Hickson has compiled a storehouse of group games and exercises, simple and direct in their approach and application. Underlying them is the possibility and necessity of tackling the deep unease and pain arising from the world in which we live.

Clive Barker
Senior Lecturer in Theatre Studies, University of Warwick

ACKNOWLEDGEMENTS

I would like to thank the wise tiger dramatherapist, Sue Jennings, my mother, for her brilliant support. She, along with Gordon Wiseman and Augusto Boal, has provided inspiration and energy, without which this book would not have been written. I especially want to thank Cath for all her help. Thanks also to Hal and Tony and to Roz, for the mother she is.

This book is dedicated to my daughter, Sophie.

INTRODUCTION

To learn about ourselves and others, people throughout the ages have gone to the theatre. We use the dialectics in theatre to help us understand ourselves, the world and our relationship with it. Theatre was used in this way before the word 'theatre' ever existed. In Ancient Greece 'theatre' was used not only for entertainment but for healing as well. The idea was that we witness or participate in dramatic performance in order to understand. Theatre as healing goes back further than the Ancient Greeks. Studies of ancient rituals in early societies show that there has always been a healing and/or a preventive element in the drama. Rituals were also associated with 'work'. A repetitive job such as chopping up wood would have involved singing or chanting. As this work was often done in groups, the whole group would get involved in the song.

Action methods have evolved from the theatre and from ritual. They are techniques used in groups for exploring difficulties and problems, or to get a group moving and active. Action denotes 'doing' as opposed to 'thinking about', 'listening to' or 'being told to'. Whenever we bring a group of people together, action methods provide us with ways of working that actually allow us to see our ideas in *action*. In other words, rather than just talking about a topic we may *perform* that topic from many different angles, so that a group can participate together in real time and unreal time (as when a few hours may represent a week), seeing ideas expressed in many different ways. Action methods equip groups with a series of versatile 'tools' that can be used in a multitude of situations.

Now I do not want readers to get alarmed with the suggestion that links exist between action methods and the theatre. We do not have to be trained professional actors to use action methods; untrained performers can use all the techniques shown in this book just as effectively as a trained performer. Theatre in its ancient sense is the capacity possessed by people to observe themselves in action. Unlike other animals we can see ourselves in the act of seeing, we have the ability to think, feel and observe conceptually, we can feel the cold today and imagine the warmth that tomorrow might bring. We can see ourselves here and imagine ourselves there, we can see ourselves in others and imagine what we look like to them.

Seeing our ideas in action

Action methods are already being used in places such as hospitals, schools and prisons, and people are realizing more and more that action methods can provide a new language to explore feelings, ideas and issues. Through participative action we can put reality under the spotlight and magnify any part of it we wish.

Learning

Action methods form a framework for running successful groups. Whatever the group wants to analyse, whether it be how to integrate back into society after a spell in prison, or stopping the boss's sexism, through to finding ways to combat bullying, getting on better with our teacher or just making our lives happier, *action aids learning, growth, self-sufficiency and self-determination*; action methods in all their forms show us a way forward and are great fun.

Enjoyment

If we relish what we are doing then it follows that we are more open to learning. If we are enjoying ourselves, learning and knowledge tend to come naturally. By using action methods we really are opening up the doors of possibility: a whole new field of ideas is available for us to use, and at no financial cost.

Finances

Not only are action methods flexible enough to suit any group as well as being a delight to use, there is no costly equipment involved. All one needs to run a group using action methods is a space within which the group can work. There are virtually no other support materials needed except for the occasional pen and paper, empty plastic bottle and mats, maybe, but then even these are optional.

In our technological society, where we are forever sitting down behind a desk, in a car, on a train or on a bus, we need action methods more than ever. The need is very great for the promotion of action methods, particularly in a society where human activity (action) is not taken seriously. I could quote the example of the people who objected about the young offender who was given a holiday. We are not automatons, even though many people in society might want us to be. There is evidence to suggest that people who are actively involved in what they are doing not only enjoy the 'task' but do it better.

Action methods are important because they give us:

▶ an active body,
▶ an active voice,
▶ active senses and
▶ an enjoyable and exciting way to explore.

Do you want to join in?

Application

Action methods are varied and very flexible. They can be used in clinical, community or social settings. They can work well with different age groups and mixed gender groups. The reader will find guidelines in relation to people's own experience of action methods which help the practitioner work within their own capabilities as well as responding to the needs of the group.

This book aims to be practical and accessible. The emphasis is on participative groupwork, good working practices, getting people involved within the group and creating new and exciting ways of learning. Participants using action methods in groups will gain in self-confidence and group awareness and will feel enabled to examine concepts, explore issues and apply skills in order to gain a better understanding of possible ways to overcome their particular problems.

In Section 1 the reader will be guided through many different approaches to action methods, including forum, image, games, exercises, psychodrama and ritual. The background of some leading exponents who use action methods, including Augusto Boal, Sue Jennings and Jacob Moreno, will be included, as will details of their pioneering work. There are quotes from and references to other practitioners, such as Clive Barker, Jerzy Grotowski and Keith Johnstone. There will also be step-by-step guides to customize your own action methods to suit your group, and yourself.

Section 2 of this book, subtitled 'Action in Action' and, following a brief introduction, divided into seven sub-sections, will take the reader through carefully selected exercises and groupwork. These practical exercises will help people get in touch with their senses, their voices and their bodies, in order for them to cultivate an awareness of themselves, their abilities and potential for change (if, of course, they choose to do so). Using action methods one does not impose ideas on a group: the group makes it own decisions and comes to its own conclusions. People find their own path within the group experience and everyone takes something away for themselves.

People are not forced into doing anything when using action methods. The doing comes naturally. People *want* to participate and they find that skills learned can be used in their work, life and studies. Participants can see that they have choices; they see that they can contribute without fear of retribution or of 'getting egg on their faces'. When action methods are being used the space becomes a safe space within which the group can work.

The appendix deals with associated therapies, providing a brief glance at a range of therapies that have elements of action in them, and talks about evaluating your groupwork. A sample evaluation sheet has been designed for you to use if you wish.

Guidelines

All of the exercises in this book have a set format: Aims, Average length, Materials and preparation, Action and procedure, Closure. With all groupwork, the leader should be thinking about (a) warming up, (b) focusing on the task in hand (c) winding down, and (d) sharing with the group.

Cautions

The group leader is the facilitator of a group. The group leader steers the direction of the group and should be fully prepared for the task. Inexperienced group leaders who work with vulnerable groups (such as people with mental health problems) should tread with utmost care, seeking guidance and regular supervision. In such group situations the group leader should focus on *building strengths* rather than highlighting difficulties.

Open up to the possibilities. Enjoy yourselves. Action stations! Go!

SECTION 1

DIFFERENT APPROACHES TO ACTION METHODS

Drama games/3
Psychodrama/4
Dramatherapy/7
Theatre of the oppressed/9
Ritual/13

Drama games

Games offer a valuable source of activity, exercise and strategy for the group leader and facilitator. Games are an essential part of human development in all cultures. Anyone can use games, since they can be used with different levels of skill, just for fun and enjoyment or with greater emphasis on promoting specific aims.

There are many people who have shown us how games can be helpful, including Keith Johnstone, with his valuable work on 'status games', Clive Barker and his 'theatre games', Donna Brandes and her 'games for teachers', and Robin Dynes with his 'creative games'. All of these people and more have shown us that games are a valuable activity. Eric Berne in his *Games People Play* has also shown us how some games can be unhelpful.

Games in the first instance help break down any initial barriers individuals might feel in a new group. They help people relax and have some fun, cobwebs are brushed away and a foundation block is put in place for the gelling together of a group. Once people are feeling more comfortable they are able to communicate more effectively, particularly with people who might be strangers.

Games stimulate the imagination, revealing a rainbow of ideas and possibilities. In the sheltered environment of a game participants can feel secure and confident — after all they are not performing, they are just playing — so growth is stimulated gradually at a pace to suit the individual. The imagination is widened and a strength is developed so that people are more willing to get involved. People become more resourceful and extend their life skills. A tree has to go through several seasons to produce its fruit. Likewise we can use games to become socially more aware as we progress from being 'grounded' to 'growth' and 'fruition'.

The possibilities that games offer should not be underestimated. More than any other way, games (particularly the 'fun' aspect) can act as the basic ingredient for any groupwork and can develop cohesion and an unobstructed, accepting atmosphere. I would go as far as to suggest that no groupwork would be complete without the inclusion of games at some level.

There is a wide range of games included in this book within Section 2. To use a word coined by Augusto Boal, many of the exercises in this book could be called 'gamesercises' — there is a fair proportion of exercise in the games and a fair proportion of game in the exercises.

Psychodrama

Psychodrama was founded by Jacob Levy Moreno. In the early part of this century, Moreno started a spontaneity programme for children and for adults. In 1909, his interest in creativity led him to encourage children to act out their problems spontaneously. This work led to development of the 'theatre of spontaneity' for adults in the 1920s. Although Moreno's work is applied mainly in clinical settings, with therapists undergoing extensive training, there is much to learn about action methods from him.

According to Moreno, the core of the self is spontaneity, the release of which is sometimes compared to a nuclear explosion. This explosion releases all of a person's creative energy. Moreno believes that on a social plane the self expands by 'retrojection', which is the process of receiving ideas and feelings from other people and identifying them with one's own. In this way we add strength to the self. Moreno believes that if this process is perfected it is possible for the person to become a genius. This self-expansion theory led Moreno to develop role reversal techniques which allow participants to see things from others' points of view. The *creative spark* that Moreno wanted to become a flame was lit when he fanned his *own* creativity. He learned two very important things: (1) that spontaneity becomes stale when its development is hidden and (2) that spontaneity can be learned. This has had a major impact on all action methods and therapies that have developed since then.

Moreno saw himself as a revolutionary:

> My vision of the theatre was modelled after the idea of the spontaneously creative self. But the idea of a spontaneous and creative self was deeply discredited and thrown into oblivion at the time when the 'idée fixe' urged me to fight its adversaries and bring the self back to the consciousness of mankind, using every ounce of persuasion and drama which I could evoke. The Vienna of 1910 was one of the display grounds of the three forms of materialism which has become since the undisputed world master of our age; the economic materialism of Marx, the psychological materialism of Freud, and the technological materialism, however contrary to each other, had tacitly one common denominator, a deep fear and disrespect, almost a hatred against the spontaneous, creative self (which should not be mixed up with individual genius, one of its many representations). (Moreno, *The Theatre of Spontaneity* p5, Beacon House, New York, 1947)

One of the difficulties that Moreno had with his theatre of spontaneity was that individuals in the audience were unable to produce true spontaneity, rather they would reply in culturally conditioned ways. Moreno lost heart with his theatre of spontaneity, particularly when some of his best actors turned their back on him and became movie actors. Moreno turned to therapeutic theatre, where he expected to get 100 per cent spontaneity from his clients with various mental health problems and psychological stresses.

In 1932, Moreno invented the terms *group therapy* and *group psychotherapy*. In 1934, he wrote *Who Shall Survive?*, which laid down the scientific foundation of group psychotherapy. In 1936, the Moreno Sanatorium was established in Beacon, New York, which became the first theatre of psychodrama. After writing several books, Moreno continued working in various associated fields, including social psychology, psychotherapy, sociology and philosophy. He became a consultant to the military services during the Second World War, and influenced the methods of procedure in military and veteran hospitals; in 1941, he established a theatre of psychodrama at St Elizabeth's Hospital in Washington, DC. In 1942, he started the Institute of Psychodrama in New York.

Psychodrama is an action method in group therapy which involves the reliving of a person's conflict with the aim of solving that person's problems. Techniques involved in psychodrama include sociodrama, psychodramatic shock and role-playing. Sociodrama is used to explore problems in relationships such as between parents and children, employers and employees, students and teachers, and police and public. Psychodramatic shock is a way of throwing the patient back into their psychological world, to explore the 'social atom' from a different angle. One can go deeper into the patient's psyche, which usually has a cathartic effect. Role-playing is the key form of psychodrama. The client, the therapist and all the assistants play out the drama of the patient's unconscious or problematic life.

Psychodrama, dramatherapy, the 'theatre of the oppressed' and radical theatre groups are committed to providing an experience that will change people's lives. Peter Brook, in his important book, *The Empty Space*, describes a psychodrama session:

> In the circle, soon, everyone will have his role — but this does not mean that everyone will be performing. Some will naturally step forward as protagonists, while others will prefer to sit and watch, either identifying with the protagonist, or following his actions, detached and critical.
>
> A conflict will develop. This is true drama because the

> people on their feet will be speaking about true issues shared by all present in the only manner that can make these issues come to life. They may laugh. They may cry. They may not react at all. But ... they all share a wish to be helped to emerge from anguish, even if they don't know what this help may be ... Two hours after any session begins all the relations between the people present are slightly modified, because of the experience in which they have been plunged together. As a result, something is more animated, something flows more freely, some embryonic contacts are being made between previously sealed-off souls. When they leave the room they are not quite the same as when they entered ... Having had a taste, they will wish to come back for more. The drama session will seem an oasis in their lives. (Brook, *The Empty Space*, p149, Penguin Books, London, 1972)

Moreno's influence over the theatre is mentioned less than his influence on psychotherapy. I would suggest that his work has had a great influence this century on people such as Sue Jennings, Augusto Boal, Peter Brook, Jerzy Grotowski and many others. Moreno's most significant contribution to theatre was his concept of the self and the creation of collective dramas based on spontaneous expression of this self.

Moreno felt his idea of returning theatre to a form similar to the dramatic enactments of the ancient Greeks was unappreciated and misunderstood. This is why he turned his attention to therapy. His influence in the therapeutic world is enormous; it includes psychiatry, philosophy, education, sociology and psychology. He was a prolific writer, applying drama to most areas of human life.

> act yourself as you never were so that you may begin to be what you might become. Make it happen. Be your own inspiration, your own playwright, your own actor, your own therapist and finally your own creator.
> (Moreno, speaking in 1971)

Dr JL Moreno died in May 1974.

Further reading

Fox J (ed), *The Essential Moreno*, Springer, New York, 1987.
Moreno JL et al, *Group Psychotherapy*, vol. XXVII, nos 1–4, Beacon House, New York, 1974.

Dramatherapy

Sue Jennings has pioneered dramatherapy and been its guiding light for over 30 years. Starting off in the theatre as a dancer and an actress she started utilizing these skills with children and adults who suffer difficulties, either physically or psychically. She took her work, as do dramatherapists nowadays, to a variety of clinical and social settings, including prison units and secure hospitals.

Drama and theatre have always had a healing function, even it would seem in prehistory. Early rituals and religious rites have many theatre components and provide a cultural context for healing. The basis of dramatherapy is theatre itself. (Jennings suggests that Shakespeare was the first dramatherapist!)

Jennings would say, "What theatre does, is that it provides a structure within which people's chaotic experiences can be contained while they are being understood." Dramatherapy is not to do with the everyday; it is to do with the imagination. There is a movement from 'everyday reality' to the 'dramatic reality', and within the dramatic reality which is the reality of the dramatic metaphor, there is a possibility for hypothesis. In the present context to hypothesize means to project ourselves into the future in dramatic form, and explore how a situation, an experiment, a formula might be. Once people have experienced in dramatic play the two realities, they are able to call upon them for the rest of their lives as a resource.

Many people get confused over the difference between psychodrama and dramatherapy. Psychodrama is very much to do with the direct issues of one's own life and, through role-play, through simulation, one can look at these — but they are specifically to do with *one's own life*. Dramatherapy establishes the dramatic distance, so that a group may use a vehicle such as a play text or a ritual or a game to explore issues. The play is big enough to contain everyone's story. Jennings says, "The paradox of dramatherapy is that distancing brings us closer ... So within the great story we all find our own story."

In 1962, Sue Jennings and Gordon Wiseman started the Remedial Drama Group (RDG) which toured schools and hospitals in Europe. It became the Remedial Drama Centre (RDC), based in North London, and was a place where performers were trained to work with children and adults with a wide range of needs and abilities. They found, as did many of the early pioneers of drama and theatre in education, that drama has a fundamental importance for people with 'special needs'; this includes people with mental health problems and physical and social disabilities. The experience of drama enables people to build self-confidence and develop communication skills, which include the ability to socialize with others. Additionally, drama stimulates people's imagination and helps them to become active in planning their own lives. It is particularly important for people with special needs to be able to develop 'self-advocacy'. New information and experience can be expressed through drama and theatre performance, which can be used to bring about social change. Drama can also act as a catalyst to bring various community groups together. This drama should include not only the need for aesthetic experience but also the development of life and social skills, the transformation of communities and, in particular, self-advocacy for those with fewer channels of communication.

After 10 years, RDC was expanded into Dramatherapy Consultants, based in St Albans. In 1976, The British Association for Dramatherapists was formed and Jennings started the first UK dramatherapy training course in St Albans. Dramatherapy training expanded rapidly and there are now seven post-graduate training courses. In 1988, Jennings set up the Institute of Dramatherapy and used as its premises a small theatre in North London. It is now part of the Roehampton Institute.

Jennings has set up dramatherapy programmes around the world, including Greece, Denmark and Israel. She has written copiously on the subject, many of her books being standard texts for dramatherapists in training. Two years spent in the Malaysian rain forest led to a PhD in social anthropology which Jennings has also used to explore rituals of healing and communal self-expression in the United Kingdom. She also set up dramatherapy in an infertility clinic, using rhythm and ritual as healing techniques. She showed that non-medical approaches could be as successful as medical intervention.

Sue Jennings has now gone back full-time to the theatre as an actress, as well as continuing some consulting work both in dramatherapy and infertility counselling.

Further reading

Jennings S, *Creative Drama in Groupwork*, Winslow Press, Bicester, 1986.
Jennings S (ed), *Dramatherapy Theory and Practice*, vols 1 & 2, Routledge, London, 1987, 1992.

Theatre of the oppressed

Augusto Boal is known throughout the world for his pioneering work in transforming theatre into a space where equal rights for all participants prevail. His development of Forum Theatre, Invisible Theatre, Image Theatre and the Rainbow of Desires has given people a new language to confront problems such as racism, sexism, depression, poor pay, homophobia and all kinds of exploitation or oppression.

The following pages, besides giving a short story of Boal's life, will predominantly be covering his work with Forum Theatre, as the techniques involved usually include action methods. Forum Theatre started its development over 20 years ago in Brazil. Initially, Boal thought it would be a good idea to go to oppressed people, such as a group of peasants, and tell them what they should do to make their lives better, or to go to a group of women and preach how to get liberty for women, but Boal was neither peasant nor woman and so had no right to tell them what to do. He soon realized this fact after he and his group performed a piece of political theatre to a group of peasants in Brazil. This play showed that the only way the peasants were going to get some land of their own and to free themselves from the oppressive aristocracy was to take up arms and fight. The play ended with the actors waving carved wooden rifles in a defiant way and they received loud cheers from the peasants who had been watching. Afterwards a peasant came up to Boal and said, "… you are right, come with us to fight". Boal was a bit taken aback and said, "I can't fight with you; these are only wooden rifles." The peasant was not perturbed and replied, "Don't worry, we have plenty of rifles for you to use." Boal at this point was a bit lost for words but eventually explained that he was an actor and not a real peasant, and that he could not fight. The peasant then complained to Boal that it was all right for him to recommend that they fight, but when it came down to it it was not his blood that would be lost!

Boal was quick to offer a different strategy in helping the oppressed when he went on to develop what he called 'simultaneous theatre'. In developing these methods Boal's one concern throughout was to help people make their own decisions for their own future, whether it be individual or collective.

Boal's Simultaneous Theatre Group would perform a scene to an audience in which someone was shown to be oppressed. Boal, acting as the joker (the joker is the facilitator, the intermediary between audience and performers, and belongs to no one party, just as the joker in a pack of cards belongs to no one suit but floats between all four), would ask the audience to suggest possible alternative routes the protagonist in the scene could take. The actors would then improvise whatever the audience members had told them. This was very effective sometimes, but problems did occur, for two very important reasons: one's words are hardly ever understood in the same way they are spoken; and it therefore follows that it is not always possible for people to make themselves understood by words alone. The following is an illustration. Boal and his group were doing some simultaneous theatre to a group of people in Brazil, about a man who had been borrowing money from his wife to build them both another house. This man was away for days at a time, returning only to borrow more money. He would leave with his wife what he said was a credit note for the money. His wife could not read. After a year or so she still had not seen the house and became suspicious. She took the credit notes to a friend for translation and found that they were actually love letters. The man had been taking money from his wife and visiting his mistress. The 'credit notes' had been the love letters from his mistress to him.

The audience were now asked to suggest possible paths the wife could take. Several suggestions were given and tried. When Boal asked for more, a woman shouted out, "Give him a strong talking to." The actors proceeded to act out the wife giving the husband a strong talking to. The woman who had given the suggestion then said, "That's not what I said; I said give him a strong talking to." The actors obliged and did the scene again making the talk much stronger. The woman who had given the suggestion was now quite angry and said, "I said a strong talking to." The actors made several more attempts at strong talking but to no avail and the woman was even angrier at not having been understood properly. Boal was now unsure how to proceed. Eventually he invited the woman onto the stage and asked her to show everyone what she meant by 'give him a strong talking to'. The woman obliged and proceeded to beat up the actor playing the husband and then she said to the same actor "Now that you've had a good talking to you can go and make my supper." The actor, alas, got a good beating and thus was born Forum Theatre.

Boal would describe Forum Theatre as a kind of fight or game, and as with all forms of games or fighting there have to be rules. As shown in the last example, it would be difficult and in fact dangerous to get anyone practising Forum Theatre if they had a likelihood of being molested. This meant that rules had to be in place. There are two unbroken rules in Forum Theatre: you cannot perform an actual sexual act on stage and you cannot assault someone on stage.

In Forum Theatre the audience are no longer spectators; they become 'spect-actors' (a mixture of spectating and participating). There is no stage: actors and spect-actors use the same space. This reduces the old division of audience and actors. The discussion takes place when the spect-actors are shown a problem in an unsolved form and are invited, by the joker, to suggest and enact solutions. The problem is always the symptom of an oppression and usually involves visible oppressors and a protagonist who is being oppressed. After the scene has been shown once (this original scene is known as the model), it is shown again to the spect-actors until somebody shouts 'Stop!'. That person then takes the place of the oppressed protagonist and tries to defeat the oppressors. This cycle is repeated as many times as possible. In Forum Theatre no idea is imposed; everyone has the chance to try out all their ideas and to rehearse them (within the bounds of theatre). It is not the place of theatre to show the correct path, but only to offer a means by which all possible paths may be examined.

Boal told the following story to me and a group of other people who attended one of his workshops in London in 1990. For me it sums up the importance of being aware of the difficulties that can arise if one tries to interfere in other people's lives by telling them what is good for them when we are not them:

> This happened to me when I was young. I was a child at my mother's. She had many hens and one day I saw that the eggs were trembling, and then comes a chick from one of the eggs. I say "Oh, she makes such a big effort; I am going to help all of the other chicks." So I got a stone and I broke all the eggs to help the chicks to be born. They were all dead except the one that had broken the egg on its own; this one was still alive. I think we as people should think the same. We cannot take an oppressed person and say, "I am going to show you what you have to do to get out of this egg; do this and that and so on", because they will be dead. But if he is able to get out of the egg himself then you are able to give him food and he is able to eat. For me it is important not to be like that, because sometimes it can be good for our conscience to say the correct things — but for whom? For what? And How?

Boal was born in Rio in 1931. His father wanted him to be a doctor. When he graduated from the University of Brazil in 1952, Boal had a degree in chemical engineering, but he was already dedicated to theatre. In 1953, he went to New York, supposedly to study chemistry at Columbia University, but mostly he worked in a small theatre on 46th Street with a group of playwrights. The writers had to direct their own plays, so Boal became a director. Returning to Brazil in 1956, he drew notice as director of the Arena Theatre of São Paulo, where he directed controversial plays. His productions at Arena included *Of Mice and Men* (1956), *Zumbi* (1956), *Tartuffe* (1965), *The Mandrake* (1966) and the São Paulo *Fair of Opinion* (1968). "I tried to do all I could to restore democracy by writing, directing and political action," Boal said. The authorities were not amused. In 1971, the Arena Theatre was attacked by thugs and Boal was jailed and tortured. After three months he was released and decided to move to Argentina, where he stayed until 1976. It was in Argentina that Boal started developing his Theatre of the Oppressed techniques. When the political situation in Argentina started to worsen, Boal moved, in 1976, to Portugal, where he directed plays and taught at the National Conservatory of Theatre. In 1978, he accepted an offer from the Sorbonne to teach in Paris. There, in 1978–9, Boal ran a five-month workshop for 20 people. At the end of the workshop he offered a 10-day session and 200 people came, so Boal divided his group of 20 into small sub-units. At the end of the 10 days it was decided to continue the work under the banner of the 'Centre du Théâtre de l'opprimé Augusto Boal'. From 1979 to this day, this has been one of the centres of Boal's activities. In 1986, after a change in government, Boal was invited back to Brazil to develop a theatre programme designed to reach poor schoolchildren. When the government changed again, this programme was extinguished. However, Boal remains based in Rio, although he travels frequently to his centre in Paris and runs workshops in Europe, Latin America, North America and Africa.

Boal is one of the giants of theatre of this century. The difference between Boal and, say, Stanislavski is that Boal's work has nothing to do with the interpretation of dramatic literature. Forum Theatre and other of Boal's methods are systems for diverting the skills commonly used in the theatre to help ordinary people overcome difficulties — or, in other words, to overcome oppressions. Boal has rediscovered for us that theatre is a very powerful tool for us to have in our bag.

"Anybody can make theatre — even actors! Theatre can be made anywhere — even in Theatres!" (Augusto Boal, *Games for Actors and Non-Actors*). Forum Theatre has been developed over 20 years and there are now many different manifestations of it in use all over the world. Every summer in Rio there is an International Festival of the Theatre of the Oppressed and there are numerous gatherings elsewhere around the world. Any community that shares an oppression can use Forum Theatre techniques to stimulate debate, show alternative solutions and to help people take charge of their own lives. They are used in schools, colleges, youth clubs, community centres, hospitals, prisons, factories and workplaces all over the world.

Like psychodrama and dramatherapy, Forum Theatre is an action method applied to bring about change. Boal has recently been venturing into politics in Brazil.

Further reading
Boal A, *Games for Actors and Non-Actors*, Routledge, London, 1992.
Boal A, *Theatre of the Oppressed*, Pluto Press, New York, 1988.

Ritual

Rituals take many forms, such as, fertility rites, initiation rites and social rites. All rituals are linked in some way to celebrations, performances and life changes. They may be part of religious rites or occur at birth, coming of age, marriage and so on. In the UK, for example, we celebrate with rituals at Christmas and Easter, even if we are not practising Christians. There is special food, gift exchange, decorations and clothes that are not part of our *day-to-day* lives. Therefore ritual is set apart from ordinary living.

It is a mistake to refer to cleaning our teeth as a ritual — tooth cleaning belongs to our everyday life as a desirable *habit*. Many people who come to groups often have a lack of meaningful rituals in their lives or have become trapped in self-destructive patterns such as rocking and head banging. These actions are sometimes mistakenly referred to as ritual instead of *stereotyped activity*. Our reaction to rituals is often exploited by the media to influence the way we think and feel about things. This is one reason advertisers are so successful: they are able to use ritual to manipulate the way we feel.

You will find ritual exercises under 'Scenes in action' in Section 2. Ritual action can be used in groups in several ways, including the following:

1. To rediscover forgotten rituals that are recalled with pleasure, such as the game of hop-scotch, or singing in a chorus or a solemn procession.
2. To create new rituals for celebrating, for example birthdays or the seasons.

3 To devise beginnings and endings of groups.
4 To build a ritual to assist someone who is leaving hospital or moving house.
5 To discover 'rituals of repair' whereby the lack of ritualization of past events can be repaired in the present.

NB Ritual can be a destructive force when manipulated by people in positions of power.

Rituals can be positive: "a safe base from which other activities can be developed. Drama can thus be considered as a means of reinforcing the known as well as finding out about the unknown. It is the ritual which gives a group its identity and which can also provide a framework for the discovery of new identities" (Sue Jennings, *Remedial Drama* p4, A&C Black, 1978).

Further reading
Coppet de D, *Understanding Rituals*, Routledge, London, 1992.

SECTION 2

METHODS AND TECHNIQUES (ACTION IN ACTION)

Introduction/17
The body in action/17
The voice in action/41
The senses in action/53
Games in action/95
Images in action/141
Scenes in action/155
Follow-up action/178
Drawing up the plan/179
A half-day introductory workshop/182
A one-hour introductory workshop plan/183

Introduction

Throughout our lives we tend to lose touch with or block the potential movement of our bodies, the power of our voices and the interplay of our senses. It is important when using action methods to be in touch with all of these.

Everybody within a group is going to be at different starting-points; no person will have the same body flexibility or voice control as anyone else. Individual senses like touch, sight and hearing will also be at varying levels of awareness. This is a fact of life in society and a fact of life when we are running a group. However, all the exercises in this book can be used with people of mixed abilities. Participants will develop from their own starting-points and will grow at their own pace. The individual will benefit and the group will benefit.

It cannot be stressed strongly enough that time spent on warming up and getting in touch with our senses will enable a group to function with dynamism, energy, passion, feeling, fun and a sense of moving forward, at a pace that suits every individual.

The body in action

We know, through sight, touch and thought, that we have a body, a head, a neck, a back and so on, but how many of us feel the size or extension of our body inwardly and directly? Close your eyes for a few moments and try to sense your entire body, bit by bit; turn your attention to every limb and part of your body. You will find that certain sections respond easily, while others remain dull and beyond your range of awareness. It is easier to 'sense' your hands, mouth or your lips but much more difficult to 'sense' the back of your head, or the base of your spine. The parts of our bodies that we use most are easier for us to be aware of, while the dull parts that play only an indirect role in our actions are probably not as familiar to us. For example, if we cannot bend our back backwards, we will not be as aware of those parts of our body which are involved as someone who can. In other words, to know one's body directly is to posses one's body, and to possess one's body means the ability to use it in action.

Our joints determine our posture because they bear the weight of our body as well as being a source of movement. Creating movement at every joint will automatically improve the way we hold and support our bodies, bringing them to a feeling of lightness and suppleness. Though we cannot make ourselves taller or shorter, rounded shoulders, drooping belly, hunched backs and many other distorted positions can be improved. Our physical build and ability to move are probably more important in our evaluation of ourselves than anything else — much more than we care to admit. Difficulty in movement undermines and distorts self-confidence, even if others do not notice it. Suppleness of joints inspires self-confidence by increasing the efficiency and aliveness of our bodies. Remember that change in our bodies has a direct effect on our psychological functioning.

As people, we are first of all a body. Our bodies house what is inside us: our thoughts, our senses, our voices. We cannot separate any of these from the rest of us. In *Alice in Wonderland*, the executioner, while trying to carry out the King's orders to chop off the Cheshire Cat's head, says, "I cannot chop off a head without a body, your majesty." We cannot have a head without a body, we cannot have a voice without a body, we cannot feel without our bodies.

It is recommended that in all groupwork we spend some time just warming up the body with some simple exercises. The following pages cover a broad range of exercises that warm up and help us get in touch with our bodies. Warming up the body should come near the beginning of any group workshop. Warm-ups should be done regularly, *they should take into account the abilities of everyone in the group* and they should be thought of as a preparation for our whole selves. They will enable us to respond instinctively, spontaneously, creatively and with ease in our groupwork sessions and in our daily life.

The exercises and games in this section not only help keep muscles supple and energized, they also help take away excess tension and lead to a relaxed and energized group. Limbering up is very important at the start of a session. An easy sequence for the group leader to remember is the 'tip-to-top' routine, (see opposite) which literally starts at the feet and works up through the rest of the body in sequence. Remember that none of the exercises are set in concrete: they are all flexible and adaptable. For example, if participants are in wheelchairs then, instead of a 'tip-to-top' routine, one might do a 'middle-to-top' routine (limbering up from the waist to the head).

Finally, a word about clothing. Of course, there is no dress code for general groupwork sessions, but loose clothing such as tracksuits and trainers are recommended.

TIP-TO-TOP

Aims: Stretching, energizing, warm-up
Average length: 20 minutes
Materials and preparation: None

■ Action and procedure

The group leader should join in a circle with the whole group. Each person should be an arm's length away from their neighbour. Standing up straight, each person should do the following three sections in sequence.

Part 1

(a) Lift right leg off the ground and, keeping the leg straight, rotate the ankle in a clockwise direction and then in an anti-clockwise direction. Repeat with the left leg.

(b) Lift right leg off the ground and, bending the leg at the knee, rotate the leg from the knee downwards in a clockwise direction (large circles) and then in an anti-clockwise direction. Repeat with the left leg.

(c) Lift right leg off the ground and, keeping the leg bent at the knee, make large circles from the hip in a clockwise direction and then in an anti-clockwise direction. Repeat with left leg.

Part 2

(a) Stand with feet apart, as wide as your shoulders, facing forwards. Put your hands on your hips and rotate the pelvis in large circles in a clockwise direction, keeping the rest of the body upright and still. Repeat in an anti-clockwise direction.

(b) Stand with feet twice as wide apart as your shoulders. Touch your left foot with your right hand, then your right foot with your left hand. Repeat 10 times.

(c) Stand up straight. Hunch your shoulders up, then down, then left up, right up, left down, right down. Repeat this sequence 10 times.

(d) Stand up straight. Stretch your right arm out in front of you. Keeping the arm straight, rotate the hand from the wrist in a clockwise direction and then in an anti-clockwise direction. Repeat with left arm.

(e) Stand up straight. Stretch your right arm out in front of you, bending it at the elbow. Rotate the arm from the elbow in a clockwise direction and then repeat in an anti-clockwise direction. Repeat with left arm.

(f) Stand up straight. Swing the right arm from the shoulder in a large circle, rotating in a clockwise direction, and then repeat in an anti-clockwise direction. Repeat with left arm.

Part 3

(a) Stand up straight with your arms by your side. Look down, look up (letting your lower jaw drop down). Repeat 10 times.

(b) Stand up straight with your arms by your side. Look over your left shoulder, look over your right shoulder. Repeat 10 times.

(c) Stand up straight with your arms by your side. Try to touch your left shoulder with your left ear, then your right shoulder with your right ear. Repeat 10 times.

(d) Stand up straight with your arms by your side. Make larger and larger circles with your head in a clockwise direction (letting your lower jaw drop down when your head is leaning back). Repeat in an anti-clockwise direction.

(e) Shake the whole of your body out.

■ Closure

At the end of this sequence discuss how everybody feels.

LEAPFROG

Aims: Energizing, stretching, body contact, warm-up, fun
Average length: 5–20 minutes
Materials and preparation: None

■ Action and procedure

Everyone in the group should stand in a line (or a circle), leaving at least a metre gap between them, bend over and put their hands on their knees. The person at the back should jump over everybody in sequence and then form the last jump at the end of the line. Then the next person does the same, and so on.

■ Variation

For groups with limited mobility, the group leader might want to think about 'walkfrog' instead. In this adaptation people would step or do small jumps over people lying on the floor.

■ Closure

Talk with the group about how this game has made them feel.

PAPER DANCE

Aims: Stretching, stimulating, imagination, body contact, creativity
Average length: 10–30 minutes
Materials and preparation: Enough sheets of newspaper for half the group to have one each

■ Action and procedure

Split the group up into pairs. Give each pair a sheet of paper. Without hands or mouths being used, the paper must be touching both partners at all times. The leader asks each pair to create a dance without letting the paper touch the ground. If pairs wish, they may perform their dances to the rest of the group.

■ Variations

Sitting dances, wheelchair dances, floor dances.

■ Closure

Talk with the group about how this game made them feel. Talk about the different dances.

BRITISH BULLDOG

Aims: Energizing, group interaction, warm-up, fun
Average length: 5–15 minutes
Materials and preparation: None

■ Action and procedure

Everyone stands against one wall, except one person who is in the middle of the room. Everyone has to try to cross to the other wall without being caught by the person in the middle. Each time the person in the middle catches someone and lifts them off the ground they must shout: "One, two, three — British bulldog." The person caught then has to stay in the middle to help catch others. The game is played from wall to wall until everyone has been caught.

■ Variation

Catchers have to hold hands.

■ Closure

At the end of the exercise, people share with the group how this game made them feel.

THAI-BOXING MATCH

Aims: Stretching, creativity, reactions, non-verbal communication, sensitivity
Average length: 2–3 minutes for each match
Materials and preparation: There should be an even number of people

■ Action and procedure

Part 1

Tell the group that the difference between boxing and Thai-boxing is that in Thai-boxing one can use the knees as well as fists. Ask the group to sit in a large circle, each person being an arm's length away from their neighbours. The first two volunteers (who should be opposite each other) stand up and begin a Thai-boxing match at a distance (that is from where they are standing — they will not actually hit each other). The two boxers will be several metres apart and must therefore simulate being 'hit' every time their partner throws a blow (try to get the participants to register the power of a blow as well). It is important that they keep the space between them, so if one person moves forward the other person has to move an equal distance back, and vice versa.

Part 2

When the first match has finished (that is, when both people have had a chance to kick the living daylights out of each other!) get them to sit down and choose two other people who are opposite each other to have a fight at a distance. When these finish they must nominate the next pair, and so on till everyone has had a go.

■ Variation

This could be done sitting down on the floor, or even in chairs.

■ Closure

When everyone has had a go, talk to the group about this game. How did different people react to different blows? Was it realistic? How did it make people feel to let out their aggression in this way? How do they feel now?

THE CRAWL 1

Aims: Warm-up, movement, improving body skills, trust, space awareness
Average length: 5 minutes
Materials and preparation: None

■ Action and procedure

Ask people to place themselves around the walls, an equal distance apart. Now get them to lie down on their stomachs, facing the middle of the room. Everybody should now start crawling towards the opposite wall with their eyes closed. If they meet someone along the way they should crawl under or over them. When they have reached the opposite wall they should turn over onto their backs and crawl back, in the same manner, to where they first started. Then they open their eyes.

■ Closure

Talk with the group about the game. How do they feel? Did they arrive back where they started? Was it difficult to crawl on their backs?

THE CRAWL 2

Aims: Warm-up, movement, improving body skills, trust, sensitivity, space awareness
Average length: 4–5 minutes
Materials and preparation: None

■ Action and procedure

Ask people to place themselves around the walls, an equal distance apart. Now get them to lie down on their stomachs facing the middle of the room. Everybody should now start crawling with their eyes closed towards a central point where they will all meet. They should start crawling over each other until a pile starts to form in the middle. When everyone is in the pile, they can open their eyes.

■ Closure

Care should be taken untangling the pile. How do they feel? Talk with the group about the different feelings they had as they crawled over people and had others crawling over them.

THE CRAWL 3

Aims: Warm-up, movement, improving body skills, space awareness
Average length: 5 minutes
Materials and preparation: None

■ Action and procedure

Ask people to place themselves around the walls, an equal distance apart. Now get them to lie down on their stomachs facing the middle of the room. Each person should move to the opposite wall without letting their hands, elbow points or knees touch the ground.

■ Closure

Ask the group how they feel. Share with the whole group.

THE CRAWL 4

Aims: Warm-up, movement, improving body skills, space awareness
Average length: 4–5 minutes
Materials and preparation: None

■ Action and procedure

Ask people to place themselves around the walls, an equal distance apart, standing on one foot. People should now get themselves to the opposite wall without letting any parts of the body touch the ground more than twice (sliding a limb across the floor counts as one touch each slide).

■ Closure

Talk with the group about the game. Did they manage to get to the other side? How do they feel?

THE CRAWL 5

Aims: Warm-up, movement, improving body skills, space awareness
Average length: 5 minutes
Materials and preparation: None

■ Action and procedure

Ask people to place themselves around the walls, an equal distance apart, lying on their bellies. People should now crawl as slowly and as exaggeratedly as possible to the opposite wall. If they meet up with someone they can either crawl over each other or around each other.

■ Closure

Talk with the group about the game. How do they feel?

HEAVEN AND HELL

Aims: Warm-up, movement, improving body skills, use of imagination, improvisation, group interaction
Average length: 30–40 minutes
Materials and preparation: None

■ Action and procedure

Part 1

Invite the group to make a circle. Start a debate about heaven and hell. After several minutes ask everybody to make themselves into an image, representing anything they have been talking about. Let everyone see each other's images.

Part 2

The group should now be divided into fours. Each sub-group is given two minutes to discuss the torments of hell and the pleasures of heaven. Simultaneously, each group now acts out the various torments and pleasures around the room. Each person must use the whole of their body in this exercise, stretching it to the limits *without hurting*. Slowly bring everyone to the centre, so that one complete writhing mass is built.

■ Closure

The group leader should ask everyone to flop to the floor and untangle carefully. Talk with the group about different aspects of the game. What did the representations tell us about how we and others feel? How do they feel now?

RACES 1

Aims: Warm-up, movement, improving body skills, energizing, co-operation

Average length: 10 minutes

Materials and preparation: A chair for each person and enough empty plastic bottles (or similar objects) for each person to have two.

■ Action and procedure

Get into pairs at one end of the room. Each pair has four bottles and two chairs. Everyone should now get on their chairs. Starting from now, no-one is allowed to touch the floor. Using the chairs, moving one in front of the other, it is a race to get to the other end of the room with the four bottles. If anyone touches the floor or drops any of their bottles onto the floor they must start again. The game ends with the last pair home.

■ Closure

Talk with the group about how they feel. Maybe it reminds them of games they didn't win or maybe at last they can win a game, or not mind if they don't!

RACES 2

Aims: Warm-up, movement, improving body skills, energizing, co-operation
Average length: 5–15 minutes
Materials and preparation: Two chairs for every three people

■ Action and procedure

In groups of three, using the two chairs, people must race from one end of the room to the other and back again without touching the ground. The game ends with the last group home.

■ Closure

Talk with the group about how they feel.

RACES 3

Aims: Warm-up, movement, improving body skills, energizing, co-operation
Average length: 5 minutes
Materials and preparation: None

■ Action and procedure

Divide the group in two. Everyone stands at one end of the room, touching the end wall. The two groups race to the other end of the room. However, when crossing to the other end, only two people from each group may touch the floor (but not with their feet). No-one else can touch the ground with their feet unless they are touching one of the end walls, and at least three people from each group must cross the floor at any one time. Except for the last two carriers, people can only stay at the finishing wall if they have got there without touching the ground. In other words, the two people who are crossing the space must carry at least one person across with them — those two will then have to go back to the starting wall. The game ends when the last person has got to the finishing wall.

■ Closure

Ask the groups to thank their carriers. Talk with the group about how they feel.

RACES 4

Aims: Warm-up, movement, improving body skills
Average length: 5 minutes
Materials and preparation: None

■ Action and procedure

People should race from one wall to the other, on their bottoms, without feet or hands touching the ground. The race finishes when the last person arrives.

■ Closure

Talk with the group about how they feel.

RACES 5

Aims: Warm-up, movement, improving body skills, co-operation
Average length: 4 minutes
Materials and preparation: None

■ Action and procedure

People race in pairs to the other end of the room. Within each pair one person can only touch the floor with their hands and arms and the other person can only touch it with one foot (they can alternate feet, but they must stay on one foot for at least five seconds at a time). The game finishes when the last pair arrives.

■ Closure

Talk with the group about how they feel.

RACES 6

Aims: Warm-up, movement, improving body skills, co-operation
Average length: 5 minutes
Materials and preparation: None

■ Action and procedure

With the group in pairs at one end of the room, it is a race to the other end. Each pair should be on all fours, bottom to bottom, with their legs intertwined. Then, like twin-crabs, they race to the other end of the room. The game ends when the last pair gets there.

■ Closure

Talk with the group about how they feel.

RACES 7

Aims: Warm-up, movement, improving body skills
Average length: 2–3 minutes
Materials and preparation: None

■ Action and procedure.

(This is a useful warm-up race if you plan to do 'Races 8'.) Everyone races from one end of the room to the other by rolling themselves across the floor. They can roll any way they like.

■ Closure

Talk with the group about how they feel.

RACES 8

Aims: Warm-up, movement, improving body skills, co-operation
Average length: 10 minutes
Materials and preparation: None

■ Action and procedure

(Some people may find this game very difficult.) Everyone should find a partner and go to one end of the room. Only one person from each pair can touch the floor at any one time. They race in pairs, from one end of the room to the other, but after every metre covered they must find a way to swap over, touching the floor (remembering that only one person in each pair can touch the floor at any one time).

■ Closure

Talk with the group about how they feel. Did anyone succeed in getting across?

RACES 9

Aims: Warm-up, movement, improving body skills
Average length: 5 minutes
Materials and preparation: None

■ Action and procedure

People should gather at one end of the room. With hands and feet only touching the floor at all times, they should slide, keeping their backs arched (like leeches or caterpillars) to the other end of the room.

■ Closure

Talk with the group about how they feel.

RACES 10

Aims: Warm-up, movement, improving body skills, co-operation, trust
Average length: 10 minutes
Materials and preparation: None

■ Action and procedure

Divide the group into two. Everyone should lie on their backs at one end of the room. Staying on their backs, and keeping one of their number off the floor with their hands, the groups race to the other end of the room.

■ Closure

Talk with the group about how they feel.

The voice in action

We all recognize that we cannot separate our voices from the rest of us. To communicate we use our whole person and not just our vocal organs. Babies can scream for hours and not strain or lose their voices. What about the screaming fan at a pop concert? They will often be left at the end of the night whispering with croaky voices or unable to speak at all. Why should the baby be more efficient about making a loud noise than a pop fan? The baby just yells at whatever is provoking it — hunger, insecurity or whatever else it might be. The baby has not learned to block its own efficient functioning, as we generally do the older we get. It is using its body the way it was designed to be used; whereas the pop fan, being older than the baby, will have adapted their body to their way of life. Now this may serve the pop fan well at a particular moment, but the long-term effects may turn out to be less than helpful. This applies to the business person, the nurse, the student, just as much as to the pop fan; in fact most of us, unless we retrain our bodies' misuse, and exercise our voices, will never be at our full potential.

People generally are not happy with the way they speak. This anxiety often compounds any vocal difficulty we may already have, such as stuttering. It is possible for most people to improve their voices with the following exercises.

How the voice actually works is tied up with muscles all over our body; it is not just localized in our vocal organs.

- ▶ Tense *stomach* muscles mean that the chest cannot fill up sufficiently, so that breathing becomes shallow as well as less controlled.

- ▶ Tension in the *jaw* restricts movements of the lips, tongue and palate, making speech less defined and controlled.

- ▶ Tension in the *back* can set up tension in the shoulders, which in turn can lead to tension in the larynx and resonating cavities.

It is important to remember that we speak with our whole body, therefore the freer the body the freer the speech.

Relaxing our body and warming up for the day ahead ensures that we shift not only tensions that block our voices but also tensions that make us feel nervous. Warming up will relieve that stress by giving our body the physical feedback that we feel okay. Here let me define what I mean by relaxation: I am not referring to lounging in a chair or watching television, but doing some relaxation exercises that gently help us free and stretch our bodies.

Breath is the power of the voice, it is the initiator of the sound, the force that hits the vocal chords causing them to vibrate. So, after a physical warm-up, it is important to do exercises that will help our breath control.

The following pages include exercises on posture, breathing, articulation, resonance and preparation of the speech organs. Short warm-up routines are included and the tongue-twisters on pp 50-51, show that exercising the voice can be fun and exciting too. These exercises are used at the start of a group session.

The group leader should regularly check with the group that they feel at ease with the exercises. Talking loudly does not mean shouting. Care should be taken when shouting, as this can damage delicate tissues in the larynx.

LOOSENING UP PHYSICALLY

Aims: To get the group ready for groupwork and/or voice work
Average length: 10–20 minutes
Materials and preparation: None

■ Action and procedure

Part 1

The group leader should join in the following warm-up, talking the group through the exercises in sequence. (Being in a circle can help, as everyone can see each other.)

(a) Stand and shake the whole body out.

(b) Stretch up to the ceiling and then flop down, bending at the waist with your hands pointing towards the floor (or touching your toes if you can stretch that far). Shake out the head and shoulders while flopped down.

(c) Slowly come up to an upright position, letting your vertebrae slot together one by one.

(d) Continue standing; keep the shoulders down. Loosen the shoulders by rolling each shoulder in turn back 10 times; then roll them back together 10 times, and finally shake them out.

Part 2

(a) Relax the head by moving it from side to side, looking over each shoulder alternately. Then move the head up and down (as in a nod). Finally roll the head around, encompassing all these moves in one smooth movement (when your head is leaning backwards *make sure that you drop open your bottom jaw*, so that you do not hurt the top of your spine).

(b) Centre your body weight onto the balls of your feet rather than your heels.

(c) Lie on the floor on your back with your knees crooked up towards the ceiling. Feel your back and spine spread in every direction possible. The group leader should take some time to allow the sensations of widening, lengthening and freedom in the different sets of muscles around the body to be experienced separately — the group must be talked through this.

(d) The group leader should go over the following with the group and get everyone to say them quietly to themselves:

- ▶ Back spread
- ▶ Shoulders spread and free
- ▶ Back lengthening and widening
- ▶ Wrists free
- ▶ Elbows free
- ▶ Neck free
- ▶ Head free

BREATH SUPPORT AND CONTROL

Aims: To improve breathing
Average length: 10 minutes
Materials and preparation: The group should have done a physical warm-up

■ Action and procedure

As in 'Loosening up physically', the group leader should talk the group through the following exercises, joining in.

(a) Breathe in through the nose to a count of three; hold it for three seconds and then breathe out through open mouth to slow count of six; relax to breathe in again. Do this six times. The more often this exercise is done the easier it is to do. When breathing out to six is mastered then breathe out to 10, 15, 20 and so on.

(b) Everyone should breathe in to a count of three and then the group should count from one to ten in a *whisper*. Breathe in again to a count of three and count out to 15. Then do the same again for 20 (if people can manage it).

(c) Repeat (b), counting at normal volume.

(d) Repeat (b) counting loudly (projecting — don't pitch voice up or shout).

TONE AND RESONANCE

Aims: To improve the sound of our voice by opening up various cavities such as those in the chest and face
Average length: 10–15 minutes
Materials and preparation: The group should have done a physical and breathing warm-up

■ **Action and procedure**

Part 1

(a) With teeth apart and lips just touching, hum gently, feeling vibration of the hum forwards over the front of the face. Do this for one minute.

(b) Repeat (a), using higher and lower notes.

(c) Repeat (a), increasing and decreasing the volume of the hum.

(d) Hum before each of these words — letting the word be placed 'forwards' in the same way that the hum is placed 'forwards'. Repeat five times.

MANY MIGHTY MEN MAKING MONEY IN THE MOONSHINE

Part 2

(a) Count from one to 10 out loud, feeling the back of the mouth lifting (as when yawning). Repeat three times.

(b) Count out loud again from one to 10, this time feeling the sound vibrating in the body and the chest (place hands on these places and feel for the vibrations). Repeat three times.

(c) Hold your nose and count from one to 10 without making it sound as if you are holding your nose.

(d) Say the following nonsense words out loud, letting the sound resonate through your cavities:

AH, AY, EE, AY, AH, OR, OO, OR, AH

Now go through chosen letters in the alphabet repeating the above *but* putting the same letter first at the beginning, then the end and then both at the beginning and at the end. For example using 'B'.

Bah, **B**ay, **B**ee, **B**ay, **B**ah, **B**or, **B**oo, **B**or, **B**ah

ah**B**, ay**B**, ee**B**, ay**B**, ah**B**, or**B**, oo**B**, or**B**, ah**B**

Bah**B**, **B**ay**B**, **B**ee**B**, **B**ay**B**, **B**ah**B**, **B**or**B**, **B**oo**B**, **B**or**B**, **B**ah**B**

SPEECH AND ARTICULATION

Aims: To help produce clear speech
Average length: 5 minutes
Materials and preparation: The group should have done a physical and breathing warm-up.

■ Action and procedure

(a) Everyone should gently massage their cheeks and their lower jaw.

(b) Open and close your mouth, letting the jaw drop open easily, repeating the words FAH FAH FAH either audibly or silently. Repeat five times.

(c) Loosen the lips and tongue by blowing kisses and sticking out your tongue.

(d) Repeat out loud the *sounds* of the following letters:

WBW (10 times)
WVW (5 times)
WVBW (5 times)

(e) Relax the jaw, with teeth apart. Take the tip of the tongue from behind the upper teeth to behind the lower teeth and repeat the *sounds* of the following letters:

LLL LLL LLL (5 times)
DDD DDD DDD (5 times)
LDL LDL LDL (5 times)

VARIETY AND COLOUR

Aims: To help make the voice more interesting
Average length: 5 minutes
Materials and preparation: The group should have done a physical and breathing warm-up.

■ Action and procedure

(a) Read the following phrases out loud with the group and let them convey the pictures vocally:

Soft snow falling
Hot sunshine glowing
Wild winds rustling
Distant drums throbbing
Brittle ice cracking
Sad voices wailing
Lovely diamonds shining

(b) Count from one to nine out loud, giving each number a rising inflection at the end of each number.

(c) Count from one to nine out loud, giving each number a falling inflection at the end of each number.

(d) Count from one to nine out loud, alternating up and down inflections with each number.

TONGUE-TWISTERS

This exercise provides a comprehensive list of tongue-twisters so that you can concentrate on particular consonant sounds. Their effectiveness when working on clarity and articulation should not be underestimated. Tongue-twisters are an enjoyable way of improving the sound of our voice. They can be used anytime the group leader feels it is appropriate to use them. *They can often be used as a good ice-breaker at the beginning of a session.*

1 Whisper the 'twisters'.

2 Speak them with teeth clenched.

3 Speak them with good tone and articulation.

4 Build up the speed of the 'twisters', still retaining clarity and articulation.

B   A baby bounces black boots with a black bendy broom.

D   "Do daring deeds, do damage," demanded Dr Dolittle's demon.

F   Freckled-faced Florence, freckled-faced Florence.

G   A gregarious gaggle of geese giggling on towards Greece, when a goose with both goggles and candour said, "Why don't you go to Uganda?"

H   How was Hal the handy Hippo hoisted happily high?

J   James just jostled Jean gently.

K   A cricket critic met with a critical crisis.

L   Lucy lingered longingly, leading her laconic-looking lapdog Lucifer.

M   Many mighty men making money in the moonshine, many mighty men making money in the sun, many were the times they made money in the moonshine, many more did they labour in the sun.

N   Nutty nodded knowingly, nurturing his nipped nicked nut.

P   Peter Piper picked a peck of pickled peppers, a peck of pickled peppers Peter Piper picked, if Peter Piper picked a peck of pickled peppers, where is the peck of pickled peppers Peter Piper picked?

Q   Quick. Whitewash the wicket quite white.

R   Around the rugged rock ruthless Rosalind ran, she ran around and round the rock until she met a man, the man was really very rude and he to Rosalind said, "Run right round Richmond park" — away then Rosalind ran.

S   The shrewd shrew sold Sarah seven silver salad slicers.

T   A tutor who tooted the flute to tutor two tooters to toot; said the two to the tutor, "Is it easier to toot or to teach two tooters to toot?"

V   Vera valued the valley's vision of Vera's violets.

W   When does the wrist watch strap shop shut?

FR   You can have fried fresh fish, fish fresh fried, fresh fried fish, fresh fish fried or fish fresh fried.

TH   Theo Thistler the thistle sifter sifted a sieve of sifted thistles into a sieve of unsifted thistles, then sifted a sieve of unsifted thistles into a sieve of sifted thistles, for Theo was a thistle sifter.

M–N   Are you copper bottoming 'em my man? No I'm aluminiuming 'em, Mum.

P–B   Peggy Babcock, Peggy Babcock, Peggy Babcock.

SH   Does this shop sell stock shot silk socks with spots on?

L–N   Nelly knits locknit knitting.

CH-SH   Stop chop shops selling chopped shop chops.

51

The senses in action

After a bodily and vocal warm-up we will be primed and ready for work. At this point it is often a good idea to get in touch with our senses. Broadly speaking, westerners take it for granted that there 'is' an outside world, which affects people through their senses, from the outside in, giving them sense impressions. They then respond to this outer world in different ways with different feelings, 'react' to it and build up an idea of what the outside world is, so that they can 'know' it. One common complaint nowadays in the west is that people are not allowed to use their senses 'naturally', to explore the world so as to experience it fully and that therefore they are deprived of many kinds of self-fulfilment. It helps us if we realize that other people who speak different languages actually seem to know different realities — it can be a bridge to another culture. The eastern view of the world and reality is almost exactly the opposite, so the eastern conception of the senses is also totally different, and the eastern view of self-fulfilment is likewise different. What the eastern tradition assumes is that we could never 'know' the outside world because what we feel or experience comes from inside: each of us 'makes' our own world.

To be in touch with our senses is to know our body, its muscles, its nerves and its relationship to other bodies, to space, gravity, objects, dimensions, distances, weights and so on. The more we are aware of ourselves the greater will be our development in any groupwork we participate in.

We tend to block off our senses, using them only minimally. I am not suggesting that this is through laziness — often it is to help us get through the day! An example would be our sense of sound. Put down this book for a moment, pick up a pen and paper and walk around the room listening, I mean *really* listen. What do you hear? Write it down. Spend two minutes doing this exercise. Depending on where you are reading this book you will, I am sure, suddenly hear sounds that your mind had blocked out, such as the gentle drone of traffic, the buzz of a generator or fridge, talking or murmuring; if you are really lucky you may hear the babble of a river or birds singing! If we were open to all sounds all of the time, we might have a lot of problems! I know that when I am writing and I become aware of external noise I have difficulty concentrating. A friend of mine has a permanently dripping tap which can irritate me very much, but he is not aware of it! When people visit me at home they often comment on the buzzing sound that my fridge makes. I am so used to this noise it is not until they make their comment that I notice it. And some people are prosecuted for their cocks crowing!

So, for whatever reason, we tend to discard much of the potential of our senses. Think for a minute about the Eskimos who, with zero visibility, navigate their kayaks rapidly along dangerous coastlines, guided by the feel of the wind and the smell of the fog, by sounds of surf and nesting birds and, particularly, by the feel of the pattern of waves and current against their buttocks. With such interplay of the senses, there can be no isolation of one sense. A hunter who relied on sight alone would return empty-handed; a traveller in remote places who ignored odours, winds and sounds would soon be lost.

The two senses that we are going to concentrate on in the following pages are sight and hearing: seeing what we look at and listening to what we hear. We end by exercising multiple senses. The following exercises are great fun and help us to open up and integrate and enhance our often dulled senses. They are recommended for use in all groupwork sessions.

MODELLING

Aims: To see what we look at, communication (visual dialogue), creativity, sensitivity, concentration, imagination, movement, group interaction

Average length: 60 minutes

Materials and preparation: In the following modelling sequence each step can be done in isolation from the others, but if there is time to do the whole sequence the participants will not only gain from each individual step but will also benefit from the transition from one step to the next. The group should be thoroughly warmed up before using this exercise. In this series it is very important that no verbal communication takes place, apart from the group leader giving instructions.

■ Action and procedure

Part 1

Ask the group to form two lines facing each other. Call one line 'sculptors' and one line 'lumps of clay'. The sculptors are now invited to mould their bits of clay into a sculpture of their choice: the sculptors move parts of their partner's body into positions (which their partner then holds) thus creating a sculpture. The sculptors may not use mirror language; that is, they cannot use their own bodies to show the image or expression they wish to reproduce. They must use touch; that is they must *mould,* down to the tiniest detail.

The group leader should let this go on as long as they feel it is appropriate. They must have a 'feel' for the atmosphere of the group. Before moving on to the next step, the group leader should be sure that the sculptor and the bits of clay understand each other. The sculptor's 'gestures' should be easily translatable (at a distance) by the bits of clay.

Part 2

The group leader should now ask the sculptors to move a metre away from their bits of clay, saying that they should continue sculpting, but at a distance. In other words, they should continue making the same movements as if they were touching the clay — they are still moulding the clay with realistic gestures. The bits of clay should respond to these gestures as if they were being touched. *The group should keep to the following guidelines:*

1. The sculptor should keep a metre away from their clay at all times.
2. No signals are allowed; that is, the sculptor should not imply through signs that their bits of clay should move this way or that.
3. No verbal language must be used (this is visual communication).
4. The bits of clay should remember to move 'at all times' *only* when the sculptor has dictated that move (for example, if the sculptor pulls the clay by the arm, the clay should fall over and not take a step forward to regain their balance).
5. As a last resort, if the clay really cannot understand a gesture of the sculptor, the sculptor can go up to the clay and use touch to show what they want. The clay should then go back to the original position and the gesture should then be repeated at a distance.

The group leader should then decide when to go on to the next stage: working with sculptures rather than with clay.

Part 3

The group leader now gets the sculptors to move further away from their sculptures, making sure that they can still see their partners' faces. The sculptors make movements and gestures to make their sculptures move up and down, backwards and forwards — almost like a remote-controlled robot, except that again the gestures must be *realistic*.

When the group leader feels that the sculptors have good control over their sculptures they are ready to move on to the next stage.

Part 4

Starting with the largest possible distance between sculptor and sculpture, each sculptor tries to bring their own sculpture together with all the other sculptures, so that they form one, multi-person sculpture. The group should try and give some meaning to the final image that is created.

The group leader can finish the sequence here if they feel this is appropriate, although there is one final stage that the group can go through, a stage at which, for the first time, an interruption in the sequence occurs.

Part 5

The group leader divides the participants into groups of five. Each group starts off with one person as the sculptor. The sculptor moulds the other four as before into a significant image, as if the sculptor was saying, "This is what I am thinking." When the sculptor has finished they take the place of one of their colleagues in the image. The swapped colleague now becomes the sculptor. The new sculptor looks at the image and then moulds a new image of their own: they alter the image of the previous sculptor so that the multi-bodied sculpture now represents something that the new sculptor wants. It is as if they were saying, "Well, that might be what you were thinking but this is what I am thinking." When the sculptor has finished they take the place of someone in the image who becomes the new sculptor. This goes on until everyone has had a go at sculpting. All the rules about touching and talking still apply.

■ Closure

At the end of this exercise, talk with the group about how they feel. What did they find difficult? What did they find easy? What was it about the exercise that made them feel in a particular way? What tricks did they find that they got up to? As the exercise progressed, how did people find the silence that they had to work in?

THE INSTITUTE OF SILLY WALKS

Aims: To see what we look at, self-awareness, trust, sensitivity, movement and improvisation
Average length: 30 minutes
Materials and preparation: None

■ Action and procedure

Part 1

Ask the group to stand in a large circle. Explain to the group that they are now going to enter the training programme for the Institute of Silly Walks. The following procedure should then be followed. Get one person to walk from their side of the circle to the opposite side and back again several times in their normal, everyday walk. While this is happening, ask the other group members to observe and comment on the walk (make sure the comments are supportive and analytical; for example: "Their shoulders are straight, their head moves from side to side" and so on). Now ask each person to walk the walk they have just seen. They should really try to feel the walk and have a feeling of becoming that person. Repeat *all* of the above with each person's 'normal walk'. Talk to the group about how it made them feel 'becoming' other people and the variation of interpretation amongst all the group members.

Part 2

The group leader should now tell the group that they have all passed the first stage and are all ready to progress to stage two. This is the same as the first, except that people now walk a walk that is not their own; in other words, they can make up their own silly walk (that should be a consistent walk) for the other group members to copy and interpret.

■ Closure

At the end of the exercise, sit the group down in the circle and get them to talk about how this exercise made them feel. Try to talk about all aspects of the way they felt, what some people saw and what others saw in different ways, and so on.

ANIMALS

Aims: To see what we look at, improvisation, building a character, movement, improving body skills, trust, communication

Average length: 60 minutes

Materials and preparation: Enough pens and pieces of paper for each group member to have one of each. The group leader should write on each piece of paper the name of an animal (horse, bear, fly, human, eagle, ant-eater, pig and so on) and whether it is male or female. Half of the pieces of paper should have the names of male animals on them and the other half should have the names of the same animals but with the indication that they are females. The above should be done without the group knowing what has been written on the paper and without their knowing that there are a male and female of each animal.

■ Action and procedure

Part 1

The group leader should hand out the pieces of paper at random, telling people that they will each have the name of an animal and that no two animals are the same. They must not tell anyone what their animal is. Ask people to find a space in the room and to start playing their animals — all at the same time. They can create this animal in any form they want: it does not have to be realistic as long as it contains the essence of that animal for them. Try to get the group to incorporate as many details as possible about their animals into this characterization (for example: wings, tail, head and body movements, how they walk, sit and so on). The group is reminded that they cannot use words at all. If people have a problem being an animal, try and encourage them to play some essence of this animal. Is it graceful? Does it lumber about? How many legs has it got? Walking on all fours could be the start of playing a horse.

Part 2

After a few minutes the group leader takes the animals into a few day-to-day activities. The group leader should tell the participants that no *actual* physical contact can be made between them.

(a) The animals are hungry. The participants should now show how their particular animal eats (voraciously, fast, slow, on the move, secretly, aggressively, and so on).

(b) The animals are now thirsty. How do they drink? (with little licks, big gulps, thinking about other things, remaining wary of other animals and so on).

(c) The animals now fight amongst themselves (a reminder should be given that no actual physical contact may be made). The participants show how they feel their particular animal manifests its rage, hatred, aggression, violence and so on.

(d) The animals are now sent off to sleep. How do they sleep? On a branch? Sitting up? In a hole? With their eyes open? Lying down? Standing up?

Part 3

The group leader now informs the animals that they can wake up and that they should go and find their mate, their partner. They must continue playing their animal while looking for their mate. When two animals feel they have met their appropriate partners they should perform a greeting ritual (again it should be pointed out that no actual physical contact may be made). During this improvised ritual everyone should stay as true to their animal's way of behaving as possible. Finally, the two animals leave the playing area and reveal their identities to each other. If they have found the right partner then they stay where they are; if not, they should both come back to the playing area and carry on the search for their mate.

Part 4

When everyone has found their partners, ask the group to form a large circle. Each couple are now invited to replay their greeting scene to the rest of the group. When people guess the identity of the animals they should shout out the appropriate animal call (a cow's moo, a dog's bark, a beetle's click, a lion's roar and so on). When the right call has been shouted out the couple return to their place in the circle and the next couple perform their greeting scene.

■ Variations

Instead of animals, use professions (still no words to be used — only sounds that are not signposts such as the repeated notes of an ambulance siren).

Feelings and their opposites.

Pairing objects.

Aliens.

■ Closure

When everyone who wants to perform the final scene has done so, discuss with the group their feelings about the game. Was it difficult?

FACE MASKS

Aims: To see what we look at, characterization, expressing emotion, movement, contact, group interaction, personal development

Average length: 40 minutes

Materials and preparation: A hand mirror, a bench (or four chairs)

■ Action and procedure

Part 1

Sit four participants on the bench facing the rest of the group. Ask each of them to make a face (not their own) and to hold the expression. Show them their faces in the mirror and tell them that they can change them if they want (the faces can be as horrible, grotesque, pure, innocent or comical as they like). The audience will probably laugh at the transformation; this is a good sign: the participants do not feel they are being laughed at but that they are making people laugh. Ask the four to retain their expressions, get up and shake hands with each other and then to say something, anything. While they are interacting the group leader should try to see if their faces are affecting their posture. If no change has taken place in their normal posture, look at their necks and see if they are tense. If so, draw a little attention to this and encourage them to let their bodies do 'whatever they want to do'.

Part 2

After a while ask the four to sit with the rest of the group. Talk to the group about these face masks and get four different group members to go and sit on the bench. Give them the mirror and tell them to pick one of the previous masks, try to imitate it and add an extra feature of their own choice. Get them to interact as before. Repeat this process until everyone has had a go (remember that the final four masks will have evolved from at least one of the first).

Part 3

Ask the group to vote on their favourite mask from the last four. This mask is then imitated by each group member, again with the added feature of their own choice. Get the group to interact with one another as this new 'being'. After a while tell the group that they are tired and wish to go to sleep; they should fall asleep where they are. When everyone is sleeping the group leader should tell them that when they wake up they will be transformed back into their original selves. Let the group sleep for a minute or so and then get them to roll over onto their sides and get up slowly and return to a circle.

■ Closure

Talk with the group about the whole experience: how it made them feel, how they saw others' transformations and how they saw their own.

WINK MURDER

Aims: To see what we look at, group interaction, communication, movement, broadening perceptions, alertness, creating characters

Average length: 25 minutes

Materials and preparation: Enough pens and pieces of paper for each group member to have one of each. The group leader, without the participants knowing, should write on two of the pieces of paper: 'You are a murderer — if you wink twice at people they die'.

■ Action and procedure

Part 1

Ask the group to form a large circle and to sit down. Ask them to call out the names or titles of people from different walks of life and write them down separately on the remaining pieces of paper. Fold and shuffle all the pieces of paper, then hand out one each to the participants. Inform them that they are going to meet at a beach party and that, as their character, they are to mingle with the other people there (the group leader should refer to clarifications in Part 2 before starting the game).

Part 2

When the beach party has been under way for 10 minutes or so, inform them that there is a murderer amongst them and that to kill them the murderer will wink at them twice in quick succession. If this happens they must count to 30 and then die as dramatically as possible. When they die they are out. The game ends in one of two ways: (a) everyone except one of the murderers is left alive or (b) both murderers are identified. To identify a possible murderer someone has to identify a possible suspect. Anyone can identify a suspect at any point in the game. The rest of the group votes: if a majority agrees then the suspect goes out of the game; if a majority disagrees or the vote is shared equally, the suspect stays in the game and the person who identified the suspect leaves the game. The people who are put out do not reveal whether or not they are the real murderers. The game carries on until the killing stops. (The group leader can check at any point to see if the two murderers have been caught, without revealing anything to the participants.) Enjoy the party!

■ Closure

At the end of the game, talk with the group about how it made them feel. Find out how they coped with the deception of the two murderers and how the first murderer felt when they were voted out and the killings carried on. Is it possible for the murderers to kill each other? Did they try?

MIRROR, MIRROR ON THE WALL

Aims: To see what we look at, sensitivity, visual dialogue, silence, movement, creativity, imagination, trust, co-operation
Average length: 40 minutes
Materials and preparation: It is recommended that the group play the game of 'Twin mirrors' (p 127) before going into this exercise.

■ Action and procedure

Part 1

Boal suggests that "we seek ourselves in others, who seek themselves in us". Split the group up into pairs and name the individuals A and B. Ask each couple to find a space in the room as far away from anyone else as is possible. The group leader identifies the As as the subjects and the Bs as the mirrors and tells them to look directly into each other's eyes. Whatever the subject does the mirror should imitate, down to the tiniest detail. Movements should be slow, rhythmical and synchronized (it is not a competition), so that an outside observer should not be able to tell who is the subject and who is the mirror.

Part 2

Once the couples have grasped the exercise, tell them that when they look in their mirror they will see the most beautiful human being. The subject will be displaying all the pleasure and happiness at seeing themselves so beautiful, and in return the mirror will be offering the same back. We will see our own image in the body of another. Someone watching this exercise should be seeing something very beautiful, with people full of contentment taking form before their eyes. When the group leader feels that each couple has struck up an affinity and movements are starting to follow on naturally (that is, that couples feel 'connected') they can take them on to the next stage.

Part 3

In keeping with this feeling of their own beauty the subject should start up a slow, delicate and deliberate rhythm of their own choice, such as tapping feet or rippling body, that the mirror imitates as before. This rhythm should encompass all that we love about ourselves and this rhythm should end up taking over the whole body. After a short time, ask each couple to swap roles and go through the procedure again.

■ Closure

At the end of the exercise, ask the group how it made them feel. Did the partners feel good and at ease with each other? Were people really happy? Did people feel really beautiful?

THIS IS MY HOUSE

Aims: To see what we look at, creativity, improvisation, group interaction
Average length: 40 minutes
Materials and preparation: None

■ Action and procedure

Part 1

Ask the group to form a large circle. The group leader should find one volunteer and say to them that without talking they can become any animal they wish and to go and nest in their imaginary home.

Part 2

This animal should then choose six other people from the group who they must model in any way they like, so that the six people form an image of the volunteer's home (the home that the volunteer would have lived in had they been that animal). When the home is finished ask the image to hold its position and the volunteer to sit down and cease being the animal. Thank the volunteer.

Part 3

Without talking about what kind of home the image represents or what kind of animal lives there, ask another volunteer to transform themselves (without talking) into the animal they believe lives in that home, and enter the home 'as that animal would'. (For example: do they crawl, walk, swing, fly? and so on.)

Part 4

When the volunteer is settled in their house, ask the remaining group members if they would like to join the volunteer there. Any that do can attempt to enter the home (assuming the character of the animal they believe to live there). *Remember that all that the group have seen so far has been images and silent representations of animals and a home; there have been no verbal affirmations of what these are.* The volunteer can let them in if they feel that this animal is one of their kind. If animals are refused entry they can either accept this fact and rejoin the circle or they can become predators.

Part 5

Can the predators entice animals out of the security of their new home? (No actual physical touch and no verbal language.) If they can, they can use these animals to build an image of their own home.

Part 6

This is a rolling game: it keeps going forwards; if a home is left with no animals in it, it decays, as do all forgotten properties. When a home decays the people in that image return to the circle. Anyone in the circle may assume the character of an animal and try to enter a home or become a predator and make their own home at any point in the game. The group leader should call a halt at an appropriate moment or when (if) content to do so and when safe families have been left with no predators lurking.

■ Variations

Use professions instead of animals.

■ Closure

At the end of the game, talk to the group about how they felt, the characterizations and what types of animals ended up in which houses. Were they all the same? Or did other affiliations come into play? How did people feel at being refused entry?

WHO IS THE MIRROR?

Aims: To see what we look at, creativity, sensitivity, movement, social interaction, improvisation
Average length: 40 minutes
Materials and preparation: It is recommended that some 'mirror' work, (such as 'Twin mirrors', p127) should already have been done with the group.

■ Action and procedure

Part 1

Ask the group to form a large circle and call for two volunteers. While the group are sitting down inform the two volunteers that they will be performing in the centre of the circle a *mirror sequence*. One of them has to be a mirror and one an initiator, but they must try to conceal from the audience which one is which. The mirror has to reflect everything the initiator does, right down to the last detail *without the audience knowing who the mirror is and who the initiator is*.

Part 2

After a few moments of action the group leader informs the rest of the group that they are going to try and find out which one is which by voting. The two volunteers continue their mirror sequence until voting has stopped. To vote, the group leader calls out the name of one of the volunteers and says: 'Is [name of person] the mirror?'. The audience votes with their hands. The same is done with the other volunteer. This voting process is continued until a unanimous vote has been reached or it has ended in stalemate. Continue the game with another pair and so on until each group member has had a go.

■ Closure

At the end of the game, ask the group to share with each other how they felt during this exercise. How did they feel while performing during the vote?

WHO IS THE LEADER?

Aims: To see what we look at, group interaction, warm-up, fun, body skills, group rhythms
Average length: 5 minutes per person
Materials and preparation: None

■ Action and procedure

Ask the group to stand in a circle and for one volunteer to go and stand outside. While this person is outside ask the group to elect a leader. The leader will now lead the other group members through different motions such as clapping hands, tapping feet, jumping, nodding head and so on. The group copies everything the leader does. The volunteer is now invited back in and asked to stand in the centre of the circle. The volunteer now has to try and guess who the leader is. The group leader should make sure that the 'leader' changes the motion regularly and that other group members are watching out for the change without giving the leader away. When the centre person discovers the leader two other people are selected to take their places and the game continues until everyone has had a go.

■ Variation

Instead of motions you could use vocal noises.

■ Closure

At the end of the game talk to the group about how this game made them feel.

WHO AM I?

Aims: To see what we look at, group interaction, improvisation, relationships
Average length: 5–10 minutes per person
Materials and preparation: None

■ Action and procedure

Part 1

Get one volunteer to leave the room. With the rest of the group decide what kind of job the volunteer has (for example, nurse, teacher, clown, butler at Buckingham Palace and so on; someone who is surrounded by a lot of activity or is in some kind of institution). When a decision has been reached, ask the volunteer to come back into the room and sit down in the centre of the room. The rest of the group, either individually or as small sub-groups, must become involved with an appropriate activity or an appropriate dialogue near the volunteer. The game finishes when the volunteer shows by word or action that they know the occupation chosen for them.

Part 2

The group leader should ensure during this game that the volunteer does *not* just try repeated guessing. Try to get them to let the character 'emerge' and to 'relate' to what is happening. They must not ask questions.

There is no urgency to discover the occupation. Let the group play with all the different characterizations that have been devised and encourage the volunteer to watch, relate and get involved. Repeat the sequence with other volunteers, until everyone that wants to has had a go.

■ Variations

Instead of jobs, use animals, or famous people, or vegetables, or patients or clients and so on.

■ Closure

At the end of the game, bring the whole group into a circle and get everyone to share their experiences of the game and how different parts made them feel.

RHYTHM SHOES

Aims: To listen to what we hear, concentration, group co-ordination, group solidarity, fun
Average length: 30 minutes
Materials and preparation: None

■ Action and procedure

Part 1

Ask everyone to take off their shoes (for comfort, and to use as a drum) and to form and sit in a large circle. The group leader should then place a shoe in front of each person. Find a song or rhyme that everyone knows and start to sing it as a group. Once a good rhythm has been achieved, keeping in time with this and the tune, each person must pass the shoe to the person on their right, except at prearranged specified moments.

Part 2

An example of this game working with 'Puff the magic dragon' would be:

Puff the	(pass the shoe)
magic	(pass the shoe)
dragon	(don't pass the shoe this time; beat it in front of the person on your right, keeping hold of it)
lived	(pass the shoe)
by the	(pass the shoe)
sea	(don't pass the shoe this time; beat it in front of the person on your right, keeping hold of it)

And so on to the end of the song. The group leader should encourage the group to get more and more precise and to work as a group rather than individuals trying to catch each other out. As the game goes on, the group can agree to make rhythms more complicated if they wish.

■ Variation

Same as above, with eyes closed.

■ Closure

The game ends when energy levels start dwindling or the group leader sees an appropriate break. Participants share with the group how they feel.

SOUND OF THE CIRCLE

Aims: To listen to what we hear, group development, vocalizations, creativity, fun, rolling warm-up
Average length: 20 minutes
Materials and preparation: None

■ Action and procedure

Part 1

Ask the group to form a circle, standing up. Talk to the group about the different kinds of noises we can make through our mouths. Ask people to make suggestions which the whole group tries out. These noises can be anything from a whisper to a scream. See how many animals the group can mimic; see how many machine noises the group can mimic; and so on. When the group leader feels that the group is comfortable with this, move on to part 2.

Part 2

One person in the circle starts with a vocalization of any kind (a roar, a scream, a squeak, a hum, a word, a pant and so on). The person on their right mimics the vocalization and then adds one of their own. This series of vocalizations carries on around the circle, getting forever longer. If a person misses any of the sequence out on their turn, the person on their right need only repeat what was said that time and add their own vocalization. The group leader should encourage people to mimic down to the last detail, including tone, volume, expression, body language and so on.

Any series of vocalizations that the group particularly likes (for whatever reason) can be chosen for more intensive work. How precise can the group get it?

■ Closure

At an appropriate moment the group leader should draw the exercise to a close and help the group members to share how this exercise made them feel.

SOUND AND RHYTHM OF THE CIRCLE

Aims: To listen to what we hear, group development, vocalizations, creativity, fun, rolling warm-up, movement, body skills
Average length: 30 minutes
Materials and preparation: None

■ Action and procedure

Part 1

Ask the group to form a circle, standing up. Talk to the group about the different kinds of noises we can make through our mouths. Ask people to make suggestions which the whole group tries out. These noises can be anything from a whisper to a scream. See how many animals the group can mimic; see how many machine noises the group can mimic; and so on. After a while try incorporating some rhythms or movements to go with the noises that are being made. For example, a roaring lion might jump as it roars or a chicken might 'peck' with its head as it clucks. When the group leader feels that the group is comfortable with this, move on to part 2.

Part 2

This game is exactly the same as 'Sound of the circle', except that there is the one added ingredient of rhythms. When each person makes their vocalizations they must add a bodily rhythm of their own choice to go with them. The rhythm changes with each person. The group leader should encourage the use of the whole body in the making of the rhythms.

Any series of vocalizations and rhythms that the group particularly likes (for whatever reason) can be chosen for more intensive work. How precise can the group get it?

■ Closure

At an appropriate moment the group leader should draw the exercise to a close and help the group members to share how this exercise made them feel.

VISUALIZE THE SOUND 1

Aims: To listen to what we hear, creativity, movement, group interaction, to prepare for 'Visualize the sound 2'
Average length: 15 minutes
Materials and preparation: None

■ Action and procedure

Split the group in two. Ask one group to vocalize a particular sound (an engine, an animal noise, a shop floor and so on). The other group must create movements that correspond to the vocalizations in some way. They can visualize the sounds in any way they like; it does not have to be realistic, it can be whatever each person associates with that sound. Get the groups to experiment with a range of sounds and movements and to swap over at a suitable point.

■ Closure

At the end of the game, help the members of the group to share their feelings about this exercise.

VISUALIZE THE SOUND 2

Aims: To listen to what we hear, creativity, movement, group interaction, contact
Average length: 40 minutes
Materials and preparation: It is recommended that the group should have already played 'Visualize the sound 1'.

■ Action and procedure

This game starts off as 'Visualize the sound 1'. When a combination of sound and movement evolves that the groups particularly like, both groups must attempt to bring everyone together (without stopping what they are doing) into one complementary, rhythmical, connected mass. Each person should be complementing the whole. When this whole is functioning, the group leader tells everyone to remember what they are doing and how they are related to those around them. The group leader now shouts, "Stop what you are doing and sit in a circle." When the group has sat down ask them to try and recreate the sound and image of the structure they have just left. How many times does this have to be rehearsed before a resemblance is achieved? Experiment with a series of different combinations.

■ Closure

The group leader should try and end the game on a suitable success and help the group to talk about the whole experience.

DEFLATE ME

Aims: To listen to what we hear, breath control, group interaction, fun, heightened imagination, movement, body skills, contact
Average length: 30 minutes
Materials and preparation: None

■ Action and procedure

Part 1

Bring the group into a circle and practise what it is like being a balloon. Individuals can inflate themselves or each other and then pull out the stopper. What happens? The whole group can be one large balloon: start off in a tight huddle with everyone blowing. As people blow, the circle gets larger and larger. Pull out the stopper. What happens?
   After a few minutes they are ready to move on to part 2.

Part 2

Split the main group up into sub-groups of four. Each sub-group should elect one of their group members to become a balloon. Each group surrounds their balloon and then pulls out the stopper. The balloon starts to deflate by breathing out and attempts to mimic the sound and movements of a balloon deflating. The other three group members should attempt to catch their balloon, plug the hole and blow it up again. The balloon should inflate at the rate at which it is being blown up. When the balloon is fully inflated the three group members should then play with their balloon (bouncing it and so on). The person playing the balloon should try and mimic as closely as possible the sounds and movements a balloon in their particular situation would make. The group leader should stress to them that they can be any kind of balloon or 'inflatable' object they like. After a while groups should swap balloons.

■ Closure

At the end of the game, the group leader should help the group members to express how they felt during this game.

GROUP HUM

Aims: To listen to what we hear, concentration, voice training, group interaction
Average length: 15 minutes
Materials and preparation: None

■ Action and procedure

Ask the group to form a tight huddle (as they do in a game of American football). One person should start to hum and the rest of the group tries to mimic the hum in all details. If anyone changes the tone or pitch of the hum from now on the others should follow in unison. No-one should try to dominate the hum; the group should try and use it as an expression of the way they feel and attempt to create a humming song, forever changing and evolving. Participants should be sensitive to the slightest change in the hum around them and get themselves in tune with it. Nothing should be planned — let it evolve.

■ Closure

The group leader should call a halt at an appropriate point and get the group members to share with each other how they felt during this game.

MOVING GROUP HUM

Aims: To listen to what we hear, concentration, voice training, group interaction, movement, body skills
Average length: 30 minutes
Materials and preparation: It is recommended that the group should already have played 'Group hum'.

■ Action and procedure

This exercise starts off as 'group hum'. When a constant has been found, the 'tight huddle' is told that they have evolved into a strange creature. They must attempt to move as this creature, while continuing to hum, as a whole, around the space, exploring as much of it as possible. When the creature is moving with relative ease, the group leader can suggest tasks that the creature should attempt, such as catching and eating prey. Decisions on questions such as 'Where is the mouth?' or 'Are we flying?' should evolve rather than be verbalized. Finally, the group leader can get the creature to go to sleep. Here the hums should continue (they could, for example, be representing the in-out breaths or snoring of the beast).

■ Closure

After a while, gather the group into a circle and get each participant to express how they feel.

COUNTING SOUND

Aims: To listen to what we hear, warm-up, sensitivity, silence
Average length: 10 minutes
Materials and preparation: Enough pens and sheets of paper for each person to have one of each.

■ Action and procedure

Hand out the pens and paper and say that for the next five minutes everyone will remain as quiet as possible. Everyone should tiptoe around the space, listening for sounds. They should write each sound on the piece of paper. After five minutes compare lists. Did the group hear sounds that were new to them?

■ Closure

Find out how this exercise made participants feel.

INTERPRETER

Aims: To listen to what we hear, trust, sensitivity, communication, self-disclosure
Average length: 60 minutes
Materials and preparation: None

■ Action and procedure

Ask everybody to find themselves a partner and go with them to a point in the room as far away from anyone else as possible. One person in each pair is going to tell their partner about something that has happened to them in their lives. The partner who has listened (the interpreter) can now ask the story-teller any question about the story they like. The story-tellers answer only the questions they choose to. After 15 minutes, bring the whole group back together. Ask the interpreters, in turn, to face the group and retell the story they have heard to the whole group as if it had happened to themselves.

■ Closure

At the end of the game, the group leader should ask everybody how they feel.

BLIND SOUND

Aims: To listen to what we hear, trust, sensitivity, communication, movement
Average length: 20 minutes
Materials and preparation: None

■ Action and procedure

Ask the group to get into pairs. Ask individuals to name themselves A or B. A should close their eyes and listen while B makes a distinct, constant and repetitive sound. Give A a minute to listen to this sound. Then ask B to move about the space repeating the same noise. A, with eyes closed, must follow B around the space, using their partner's sound as a guide. If B stops making the sound then A must stop moving. B must guide A, with the sound only, around the space, being careful not to let A bump into walls or other people. After a while get each pair to swap their roles so that all the As take the Bs on a journey around the space.

■ Closure

The group leader should call a halt at an appropriate place and talk about the game with the group. How did people feel when they were blind? Were people confused by the sounds from other pairs? Did anyone end up following another person's sound?

WHO SAID 'ARGHH'?

Aims: To listen to what we hear, group interaction, movement
Average length: 20 minutes
Materials and preparation: None

■ Action and procedure

Everyone should close their eyes and wander about the space with arms folded in front of them and hands over the elbows. If people wander about slowly like this around the space and if they bump into others or a wall they should come to no harm. The group leader designates a person by touching them on the shoulder to say 'Arghh' in any way they like. The rest of the group must try to work out who it was. When an agreement has been reached as to who said 'Arghh', the game starts again.

■ Closure

The group leader should find out how group members feel after playing this game.

BLIND CATCH

Aims: Dynamizing several senses, contact, breaking down barriers, fun
Average length: 20 minutes
Materials and preparation: None

■ Action and procedure

Ask everyone to close their eyes and fold their arms in front of them with their hands covering their elbows. They then begin to move around the space slowly, without talking. When they meet people they should greet them without words and move on. After a while the group leader suggests several tasks for each person to undertake, still with their eyes closed, using touch to explore:

(a) Find people the same height as you and 'stick' to them.

(b) Find people with hair as long as yours.

(c) Find people with a face like yours.

(d) Find people wearing a similar top to yours.

(e) Suggest other tasks (for example, to do with hands, jewellery, clothes).

(After some time the collected groups may open their eyes and check their choices.)

■ Closure

Talk with the group about how they feel after playing this game.

BLIND RETURN

Aims: Stimulating several senses, contact, movement
Average length: 20 minutes
Materials and preparation: None

■ Action and procedure

Part 1

Everyone is asked to fix their gaze on any place in the room. They then close their eyes, stretch their arms out in front of them and walk slowly to the place they had elected. Eyes must not be opened until they feel that place has been reached (even if they bump into other people). Do this three times. How close did people get?

Part 2

Ask everyone to find a partner and hug them. In mid-embrace they must close their eyes, release from the hug, walk backwards a prearranged number of steps and then retrace their steps to hug their partner again. Do this three times. Did people end up hugging the right partners?

Part 3

Ask everyone to find a different partner and shake their hands. In mid-handshake they must close their eyes, release from the shake, walk backwards a prearranged number of steps and then retrace their steps to shake hands with their partner. Do this three times. Did they end up shaking hands with the right partners?

■ Closure

At the end of the game, talk to the group about how it made them feel.

THE MAGNET

Aims: Dynamizing several senses, contact, movement
Average length: 15 minutes
Materials and preparation: None

■ Action and procedure

Ask everyone to close their eyes and fold their arms in front of them with their hands covering their elbows. They then begin to move around the space slowly, without talking. The group leader calls out that the magnet is negative: if they collide with anyone they must back off quickly. Everyone tries to avoid touching anyone else. After a while the group leader calls out that the magnet is now positive: if anyone accidentally touches they must now stay stuck together for several seconds, still walking (people might have to end up walking backwards or sideways). After a while the group leader should say, "Stay stuck". People should now stay stuck to anyone they touch, still walking. Will the whole group stick together?

■ Closure

At the end ask everyone to open their eyes and see who they are stuck to. Help group members to share with each other how they felt about this game.

GOALKEEPER

Aims: Dynamizing several senses, trust, fun (scary), group interaction, energy building
Average length: 15 minutes
Materials and preparation: None

■ Action and procedure

Ask six people to stand at one end of the space in two lines, close together. They should be facing the other end with their arms stretched out to the side. They are acting as goalkeepers to the rest of the group. Ask the rest of the group to stand at the other end of the space and, one at a time, to close their eyes and run as fast as they dare, taking care if they are heavy, to the goalkeepers. They should keep their eyes closed all the time and not slow down their run. The goalkeepers will catch the runners round their waists. Let each person have several tries, but do not force them to do it. After a while, change goalkeepers and let others have a go.

■ Closure

Talk with the group about how this game made them feel.

BLIND SLALOM

Aims: Dynamizing several senses, movement, concentration
Average length: 20 minutes
Materials and preparation: None

■ Action and procedure

Get five people to position themselves in a line, one metre away from each other, in the centre of the space. The rest of the group, one-by-one, must position themselves at one end of the line and then in turn slalom (with eyes closed) around the five, *no faster than walking pace*.

■ Variation

Try blind figure of eights around two people.

■ Closure

Talk to the group about how this game made them feel.

FEEL THE OBJECT

Aims: Dynamizing several senses, sensitivity, fun, concentration
Average length: 20 minutes
Materials and preparation: Several objects, such as a shoe, a pen, a ball, a bottle, a book

■ Action and procedure

An object is passed to a participant who has their eyes closed and hands behind their back. By touching the object with other parts of their body, this person has to try and guess what it is. After each person in turn has had a go, try giving people two objects to identify.

■ Closure

At the end of the game, help group members to share with each other how they feel after playing this game.

HAT AND RUN

Aims: Dynamizing several senses, movement, warm-up, fun
Average length: 20 minutes
Materials and preparation: A hat or similar object

■ Action and procedure

Split the group into two teams facing each other, about four metres apart. The hat should be placed in between the two teams. Each team elects a member to go and get the hat (only one person from one team at a time). If an opposing team member touches them while they are holding the hat, they must drop it. Each person must try and get the hat back to their team without being touched. The first team to score nine wins.

■ Closure

Talk with the group about how they felt playing this game.

Games in action

Facilitators and teachers will know that the absence of supervised games in a lesson will often result in the manifestation of unregulated play. Notes being sent around the classroom, paper pellets being thrown at the teacher's back and scribbling on desks are a few examples of this less creative play. As people we need play; it is an important part of our learning process, both as adults and as children. Organized games are fun because they have rules and help us direct our energies in a positive way.

Playing a game makes sure that people are being active rather than passive. A game can break the ice in any workshop — it involves participants in a joint activity without any individual feeling the pressure of having to 'perform' in front of the rest of the group. Having a back-up selection of games can also pull the group out of a tight spot if the leader is stuck, or if the workshop has suddenly gone stale or has come up against unforeseen barriers. A game in these situations can keep energies flowing, explore difficult areas and give the facilitator time to get the workshop moving in the right direction again.

Playing brings people together, no matter how diverse their backgrounds or training. Games are a dialogue, not necessarily verbal, between people. This dialogue takes the participants on a journey, often into the unknown. To play the game the group must know the boundaries within which the game is played — the rules. It is possible for the group to make its own rules and all the games in this book can be adapted to this effect. The facilitator must be sure that everyone knows the rules, explain them slowly and clearly and, if needs be, have a practice before the game is played properly.

Games in a multitude of forms are played all over the world. In what follows I have concentrated on active games rather than sitting and writing games. I have divided them into two groups. The first comprises warm-ups, starters and closures, the second games which can be used to help us get in touch with our senses, our bodies and our understanding of ourselves and others. Games can be used independently or in conjunction with other games and exercises. Do not be frightened of experimenting.

'Games in action' can be dipped into and does not need to be read as a whole. The details for each game have been written independently of each other so as to allow you to have on a single page or a few pages all the information (such as preparation, materials, benefits and so on) needed to run any particular game.

The only things taken for granted are that you already have a space within which to work and a group to work with.
Enjoy your playing.

Pages 97–107	Warm-ups, Starters & Closures
Pages 108–140	Games for when you have warmed up

WHAT'S IN A BOTTLE?

Aims: Ice breaking, stimulating imagination
Average length: 10 minutes
Materials and preparation: A large empty plastic bottle

■ Action and procedure

Ask the group to form a circle in the middle of the room, with each person being about two shoulder widths apart. Join the circle yourself before you explain the rest of this game: the plastic bottle you are holding in your hands *is no longer a plastic bottle*; it can now become whatever they want it to become. Explain that you want people, in turn, to *mime* what the bottle has become in their hands. Then mime a suggestion yourself, such as putting the bottle on your head and saying to the group: "Now it has become a hat." After each mime make sure that you or the group have guessed what the bottle has become in their hands *before* it is passed to the next participant and have said what it is to the whole group. The game finishes when the bottle comes full circle back to you. If people have difficulty thinking what to mime, just remind them that it can become anything they want in the whole world: there is no right or wrong answer.

■ Closure

Participants share with the group how they feel.

CATCH MY NAME

Aims: Introductions, memorizing
Average length: 20 minutes
Materials and preparation: One ball for every group of 16 people

■ Action and procedure

Ask the group to sit in a circle. Pass the ball around the circle. When someone receives the ball they must say their first name clearly and then pass the ball on. When everyone has been named and the ball is back at the beginning, the person holding the ball can throw it to any other participant. The catcher must say the thrower's name. The ball is then thrown to someone else who must say that thrower's name, and so on. If a person cannot remember the name of a person who has thrown to them, they must ask and repeat the name before continuing with the game. The game ends when everyone can remember the names of all the people in the group.

■ Variations

The thrower must say the name of the person they are throwing to. The catcher must say the thrower's name *and* the thrower must say the catcher's name.

■ Closure

Participants share with the group how they feel.

SALT AND PEPPER

Aims: Ice breaking, concentration, fun
Average length: 20 minutes
Materials and preparation: Two small objects, such as a pen and a rubber

■ Action and procedure

Part 1

The group form a circle, sitting down. The leader has a pen and a rubber. The leader passes the pen to the right saying, "This is the pepper." Player 1 says, "The what?" The leader says, "The pepper." Player 1 says, "Ah, the pepper" and then takes the pen. Player 1 turns to player 2 on their right and says, "This is the pepper." Player 2 says, "The what?" Player 1 turns to the leader and says, "The what?" The leader says, "The pepper." Player 1 turns back to player 2 and says, "The pepper." Player 2 says, "Ah, the pepper" and then takes the pen. Player 2 then turns to player 3 on their right and says, "This is the pepper." Player 3 says, "The what?" Player 2 turns to player 1 and says, "The what?" Player 1 turns to the leader and says: "The what?" The Leader says, "The pepper." Player 1 turns to player 2 and says, "The pepper." Player 2 turns to player 3 and says, "The pepper." Player 3 says, "Ah, the pepper" and then takes the pen. Player 3 turns to player 4 on their right and says: "This is the pepper."

Part 2

Part 1 continues all the way round the circle until the pen is back in the leader's hands, with the "The what?" always being passed back to the leader and the "The pepper" always being passed back to the person being offered the pen before they take it. When this has been practised a few times, start again, and at the same time pass the rubber in the opposite direction, calling it the salt. Great confusion occurs when the salt and pepper come to the people sitting opposite the leader in the circle. This is encouraged and acceptable.

■ Variation

Let other group members start the game, holding the salt and pepper.

■ Closure

At the end of the exercise ask each participant how they felt (share feelings).

THE CROSS AND THE CIRCLE

Aims: Ice breaking
Average length: 5 minutes
Materials and preparation: None

■ Action and procedure

Ask the participants to describe a circle with their right hand. It is easy, everyone can do it. Tell them to stop. Now ask them to describe a cross with their left hand. Even easier! Tell the group to stop. Now ask them to do both at the same time. It is almost impossible.

■ Variation

Ask the participants to describe a circle with their right foot. Stop. Ask them to draw their first name in the air with their right hand. Stop. Now do both together. This again is almost impossible to achieve. The reasons are purely psychological, as there are no physical obstacles. With practice it can be done.

■ Closure

Check with the group that everyone felt at ease with this exercise.

FILL THAT SPACE

Aims: Awareness, energy building
Average length: 5 minutes
Materials and preparation: None

■ Action and procedure

Ask the participants to walk quickly (or run slowly) around the room, filling up any space that they see. They must jump into a space when they see it, but not stay there, keeping on moving around the room. They must be aware of each other and the space, not bumping into each other or the walls. The leader lets this go on for a little while and then shouts out "Stop!" All the participants must freeze where they are. The idea is that they should all be spread around the whole floor space equally. The leader at this point could make them aware of any empty spaces left around the room. Repeat this several times.

■ Variations

When the leader tells them to stop, everyone must touch one other person in the room (without moving from the spot). When the leader tells them to stop, everyone must touch two people in the room (without moving from the spot).

■ Closure

Participants share with the group how they feel.

HOW YER DOIN'?

Aims: Introduction, integration, awareness
Average length: 5 minutes
Materials and preparation: None

■ Action and procedure

Each participant must say "How yer doin'?" to all the other participants, at the same time shaking hands with them. Everyone must always be shaking hands with someone. Before anyone can disengage from a handshake, they must start up a handshake with someone else. This means that some people may be shaking hands with two people and unable to let go until one of them finds another partner to shake hands with.

■ Variation

Use different greetings.

■ Closure

At the end of the exercise, ask each participant how they felt (share feelings).

WHAT WAS I DOING?

Aims: Closure, memorizing
Average length: 20 minutes
Materials and preparation: None

■ Action and procedure

Ask participants to find a space away from anyone else and to sit down. Tell them that this game requires no talking; it is purely mime. The leader will now call out every few minutes a date and a time. Participants have to think what they would be doing at that time on that day and mime their actions. Take the group through a typical working day and night. See how this compares with weekends and special occasions such as celebrations. Spend about 20 minutes doing this, ending with everyone miming sleep.

■ Variations

Mime a journey or a holiday.

■ Closure

Ask participants to get up in their own time. It is often a good idea to follow this exercise with 'Recap' (next exercise).

RECAP

Aims: Closure, relaxation
Average length: 10 minutes
Materials and preparation: None

■ Action and procedure

Ask the group to lie down on their backs, with their knees crooked towards the ceiling, with each participant being as far from anyone else as possible. Tell them to close their eyes. The leader must now talk the group through a body relaxation, starting with the toes, then the feet and then the ankles, and so on up through the entire body, releasing the stress and tension in the muscles as they go. The leader then asks them to picture the group session in their mind's eye and to remember all the different things that have happened. It can be a good idea for the leader to read to the group a list of all the things they have done that session.

■ Variation

Add in some breathing exercises.

■ Closure

Allow people to get up in their own time, reminding them to roll onto their sides first and not to get up too quickly as this will make them dizzy.

BACK TO SELF

Aims: Deroling, closure
Average length: 10 minutes
Materials and preparation: None

■ Action and procedure

This should be done after role-playing exercises and can be used at the end of a session. Ask participants to visualize the character(s) they have just played. That character should then be visualized walking away down a path, round a corner and waving goodbye before being lost to sight. Once this is done, participants can share with each other what their other roles were like. If any of those roles are still with them, they should talk about it with the group and decide which aspects of that character to give up and which to absorb.

■ Variation

Leave the character standing and walk away oneself.

MASSAGE CIRCLE

Aims: Relaxation, closure
Average length: 5 minutes
Materials and preparation: None

■ Action and procedure

Ask the group to sit in a tight circle. Ask them to turn to the person on their left. You should now have a circle with everyone facing someone else's back. Ask participants to gently massage the shoulders of the person in front of them. After a few minutes tell them to turn to the person on their right and do the same again.

■ Variations

Massage the head of the person in front. Face to face: participants massage each other's faces. *For a simple version, they can massage each other's hands.*

MUSCLES

Aims: Trust building, concentration, feeling what we touch
Average length: 10 minutes
Materials and preparation: None

■ Action and procedure

Split the group into pairs. Get each pair to face each other and hold each other's shoulders. They must try and push one another away with all their strength, but no-one must win and no-one must give way.

■ Variation

Use bottoms, sitting back to back.

■ Closure

At the end of the exercise, ask each participant how they felt (share feelings).

MINIMUM SURFACE CONTACT

Aims: Exploration, body/gravity awareness, feeling what we touch
Average length: 10 minutes
Materials and preparation: Suitable wooden floor (not concrete)

■ Action and procedure

Tell participants that they must get the whole of their bodies to touch the floor *but only a little bit at a time*. This must be done slowly and carefully, with participants all the time being aware of countering the force of gravity.

■ Variation

As above, but linking up with one person, then two, then three and so on. Strictly no talking!

■ Closure

At the end of the exercise, ask each participant how they felt (share feelings).

SLOW-MOTION RACE

Aims: Teamwork, stimulating dormant muscles, feeling what we touch
Average length: 10 minutes
Materials and preparation: None

■ Action and procedure

Everyone starts from one end of the room and races to the other end. The winner is the last one there. Everyone must take the largest steps they can, in slow motion, without interrupting their movements (that is, the motion must be continuous). Both feet can never be on the ground at any one time.

■ Variations

In pairs linked together (the partners sit on the ground and interlock legs), race the length of the space in slow motion. Pairs race as above, but standing back to back, with interlocked arms.

■ Closure

At the end of the exercise, ask each participant how they felt (share feelings).

OBJECT BALANCE

Aims: Creativity, balance, feeling what we touch
Average length: 20 minutes
Materials and preparation: Enough objects (such as a ball, a chair, a case, a pencil, a plastic bottle) for each participant to have one.

■ Action and procedure

Give each participant an object. They must try to find as many ways as possible to hold their object: with their feet, with their backs, in their teeth, with their knees, far from the body, near the body and so on.

■ Closure

At the end of the exercise, ask each participant how they felt (share feelings).

BLIND FACE

Aims: Trust, sensitivity, feeling what we touch
Average length: 2 to 5 minutes per person
Materials and preparation: A blindfold (optional)

■ Action and procedure

Ask the group to form a circle and get one participant to go in the centre wearing a blindfold or closing their eyes. The leader should then swivel the blindfolded person in the centre to disorientate them. The blind person then moves forward with arms outstretched until they come to a person in the circle. They explore the face of this person with their hands and then try to guess who it is. Once they have guessed, they take off the blindfold, see if they were right and give the blindfold to that person. The new blindfolded person goes through the same procedure.

■ Variation

The whole group close their eyes and then find a partner. Keeping their eyes closed, each pair explores their partner's face.

■ Closure

The game ends when everybody has had at least one turn at being blindfolded. At the end the leader should ask everyone how this game made them feel and share these experiences with the group verbally or non-verbally.

CARNIVAL TIME

Aims: Awareness, sharing, listening to what we hear
Average length: 20 minutes
Materials and preparation: None

■ Action and procedure

Split the group into lines of three. Each person in each group of three takes it in turn to lead their group in a bodily and verbal rhythm, which the other two copy. Each group then chooses a rhythm out of the three for their group to perform. Allow a parade of groups, like floats at a carnival, and then give everybody the chance (several times) to change to other groups if they prefer their rhythms. When joining another group a person must mimic the bodily and verbal rhythms of the group they are joining. Make sure the whole space is being used (groups do not need to stay rooted to the spot — encourage them to move around). As groups change some will get bigger, some smaller and some will disappear. If a group gets down to only one person, that person must join another group.

■ Closure

At the end the leader should ask everyone how this game made them feel and share these experiences with the group verbally or non-verbally.

HOT SEAT 1

Aims: Self-validation, group development, memorizing, listening to what we hear
Average length: 2 minutes per person
Materials and preparation: A chair

■ Action and procedure

A chair is placed in front of the group. Each person in turn is invited to sit on the chair and talk to the group on a topic that interests them.

■ Closure

At the end the leader should ask everyone how this game made them feel and share these experiences with the group verbally or non-verbally.

HOT SEAT 2

Aims: Self-validation, group development, memorizing, listening to what we hear, seeing what we look at
Average length: 2 minutes per person
Materials and preparation: A chair

■ Action and procedure

Split the group into sub-groups of 10. A chair is placed in front of each sub-group. Each person in turn is invited to sit on the chair and talk to the group on a topic that interests them. When everybody has had a turn, split the group into pairs. Each person in turn sits in the chair again and as far as possible imitates the words and the actions of their partner's hot seat performance.

■ Variation

The leader chooses a topic that everyone talks about, such as: 'Why did I attend this workshop?' Time can be increased as necessary.

■ Closure

At the end the leader should ask everyone how this game made them feel and share these experiences with the group verbally or non-verbally.

CHANGE THE PRESIDENT

Aims: Expression, communication, sharing, listening to what we hear, seeing what we look at
Average length: 30 minutes
Materials and preparation: None

■ Action and procedure

Split the main group into groups of five and ask each to nominate a president. The other four become the president's bodyguards. Each group then takes up the following positions: the president in the centre, one person directly behind, facing the back of the president, one person either side of the president, facing the same way as the president and one person in front, facing the president. Each group now has a diamond shape. The bodyguards are all about two feet away from the president. Whatever the president now does, the guards mimic; encourage sounds, action and movement. The bodyguard facing the president mimics as if they are a mirror. Every now and again the leader should shout, "Change the president!", whereupon all five move one place, so that now there is a new president in each group. Continue until everyone has had a chance to be president.

■ Closure

What was it like to be president? What was it like to be a bodyguard? How do people feel?

PER TO PER

Aims: Enhanced imagination, interaction, body skills
Average length: 10 minutes
Materials and preparation: None

■ Action and procedure

Split the group into pairs. The leader now calls out names of parts of the body, which each pair must join; for example, "nose to nose" — each pair must now put their noses together — or "palm to knee" — each pair must join a palm and a knee. The leader makes it as easy or difficult as they see fit and ends the game by saying "per to per", which means the pairs should separate.

■ Variation

Make the body contacts cumulative: when partners have put two parts of their bodies together they must keep them there while carrying out the next instruction (up to a maximum of five or six).

■ Closure

At the end the leader should ask everyone how this game made them feel and share these experiences with the group verbally or non-verbally.

WALKING MILLIPEDE

Aims: Co-ordination, contact, team spirit
Average length: 15 minutes
Materials and preparation: A chair

■ Action and procedure

A person sits on the chair with their legs pressed tightly together; a second person sits on their lap, with the other's arms around their waist; a third person sits on the second person's lap, and so on, everyone holding the waist of the person in front and with knees held tightly together. The leader starts a chant which the group copy in unison: "left, right, left, right" and the group first move their left legs forward and then their right legs, in time with the chant. The chair is no longer needed and the group leader should take it away. See how much of the space this walking millipede can explore.

■ Variation

The person at the front of the line must try to put their knees under the bottom of the person at the other end of the line, thus forming a circle. Everyone can now let go of each other's waists as there is no longer a need to hold each other.

■ Closure

At the end the leader should ask everyone how this game made them feel and share these experiences with the group verbally or non-verbally.

FOLLOW THE PALM

Aims: Communication, sensitivity, creativity, seeing what we look at
Average length: 15 minutes
Materials and preparation: None

■ Action and procedure

Split the group into pairs. Name each partner A or B. A must put his or her palm 5 inches or so (12 cm) from B's face. Wherever A now puts his or her palm, B must follow, keeping the same distance from palm to face. A now takes B on a journey around the space. People must be aware of their partner's capabilities and try to take them a little bit beyond them. Encourage people to use the vertical space as well as horizontal space. Swap over A and B, then change partners.

■ Variation

Split the group into threes: A, B and C. A puts up both palms, B and C each put their faces 5 inches or so (12 cm) from one of the palms. A takes B and C on a journey around the space.

■ Closure

At the end, the leader should ask everyone how this game made them feel and share these experiences with the group verbally or non-verbally.

THE GAME OF POWER

Aims: Understanding images, power relationships, taking and losing control, seeing what we look at
Average length: 60 minutes
Materials and preparation: One table, six chairs and an empty plastic bottle placed in a pile in the middle of the space

■ Action and procedure

Part 1

Ask the group to form a circle around the pile. Now ask one person in the group to go into the centre and arrange the items into an image of power, making one of the chairs the most powerful item in it. They can put the chairs, table and so on on their sides, backs, on top of each other, however they want, as long as they keep everything within the circle. Now talk to the group about which chair they think is the most powerful. Ask someone else to make a different image with the items, still making one chair the most powerful in relation to the others. Talk again about this image. Carry on until you have seven or eight different images and then let the group decide on one image to work on, one that everyone agrees represent 'power' with one chair being the most powerful in relation to all the others.

Part 2

Set up the image from part 1. Remind people that whatever follows in this game must be played within the circle. Now ask one person to place themselves in the image, making them the most powerful person, and then freeze in position. Check with the rest of the group whether they agree that they are the most powerful (do not change the image). Ask a second person to put themselves in the image, trying to take all or some of the power away from the first (they must not move the first person). They also freeze in position. Keep talking to the group about what kind of power they are seeing and who they think is the most powerful. Get a third person up and into the image, then a fourth, and so on, with each successive person trying to make themselves the most powerful person in the image. The game ends, leaving an image of power.

■ Closure

Talk with the group about the different forms of power they have seen. At the end the leader should ask everyone how this game made them feel and share these experiences with the group verbally or non-verbally.

FLYING TO THE MOON

Aims: Role-playing, use of imagination, group decision-making
Average length: 40 minutes
Materials and preparation: None

■ Action and procedure

Divide into groups of eight. Ask each group member to adopt a specific role such as a doctor, a mechanic, a pilot and so on (these can be picked from a hat). Tell groups that a huge meteor is about to hit the earth and the only way of escape is in a rocket about to fly to the moon. There is only enough room in the rocket for six people and therefore two members cannot go. The group must decide who is left behind; each member should argue as to why they should be allowed to go. No murders are allowed. Set a time limit for the decision. At the end discuss how the group reached their decision, whether members were active or passive in the decision-making process and so on.

■ Variation

Use different scenarios such as a desert island or an air raid shelter, or use famous people.

■ Closure

The leader should ask everyone how this game made them feel and share these experiences with the group verbally or non-verbally.

HOW MANY As IN ONE A?

Aim: Creativity, use of imagination, voice skills, group interaction, communication, listening to what we hear
Average length: 40 minutes
Materials and preparation: None

■ Action and procedure

Ask the group to form a circle. A volunteer goes into the middle of the circle and expresses an emotion, a feeling or an idea, using only the sound of the letter 'A'. They must accompany this sound with a physical gesture or movement. Everyone else in the circle must repeat (as a group) the sound and gesture three times. Then someone else goes into the middle and expresses a different emotion, feeling or idea, with a gesture, still just using the sound of the letter 'A'; the whole group again repeats three times. This goes on until everyone has gone into the circle and expressed their 'A'. Now they go on to 'E', 'I', 'O', 'U'.

■ Variation

Instead of vowels use words or sentences.

■ Closure

At the end the leader should ask everyone how this game made them feel and share these experiences with the group verbally or non-verbally.

THE BLIND CAR

Aims: Trust, sensitivity, interaction, dynamizing several senses
Average length: 20 minutes
Materials and preparation: None

■ Action and procedure

Part 1

Ask the group to split up into pairs and name themselves A and B. A closes their eyes and becomes a blind car, B stands behind A and is the driver. B steers A by pressing a finger on A's back: middle of back is straight on, left shoulder is left, right shoulder is right (the nearer the shoulder the sharper the bend), hand on neck is reverse. The speed of the car is regulated by softer or harder pressure with the finger and the car is stopped when the driver stops touching them. Participants must take care not to bump into other cars, walls and so on and must not talk to each other.

Part 2

Ask pairs to explore as much of the space as possible, park their cars, go on motorways and so on. Partners swap roles after a few minutes.

■ Variation

Form a blind train with several blind cars joined together, the driver at the back; each successive blind carriage has to translate the driver's instruction to the carriage in front. Passing through several carriages, these physical messages must be translated by the person at the front of the train who is the blind locomotive.

■ Closure

At the end the leader should ask everyone how this game made them feel and share these experiences with the group verbally or non-verbally.

THE VAMPIRE OF STRASBOURG

Aims: Understanding oppression, concentration, contact, group interaction, listening to what we hear
Average length: 25 minutes
Materials and preparation: None. 'To vampirize' means 'to turn someone into a vampire'.

■ Action and procedure

Part 1

This game can be great fun and also quite startling, as the title may suggest. The leader asks everyone to close their eyes, stick their elbows out in front of them with right hand over left elbow and left hand over right elbow, and then to walk carefully around the room. The leader then squeezes the back of someone's neck and that person becomes the first 'vampire of Strasbourg' — their arms extend in front of them and they give a scream of terror. The vampire, still with eyes closed, must now seek out other necks in order to vampirize them.

Part 2

Each time the vampire finds a neck and squeezes it as the leader did, successive victims scream in terror as they are vampirized, their arms rise in front of them and they join in the hunt to vampirize. If a vampire squeezes the neck of another vampire then this person is rehumanized and lets out a scream of sheer pleasure. Participants must try to flee the most vampire-infested areas, listening to the screams of terror as people are vampirized but also to the screams of pleasure because, although someone is rehumanized there must be a vampire next to them! People must keep their eyes closed the whole time.

■ Closure

At the end the leader should ask everyone how this game made them feel and share these experiences with the group verbally or non-verbally.

NB I first played this game in the late 1980s at a workshop run by Augusto Boal in London. We all found it strange how people liked being vampirized: instead of running away they could now persecute others as a vampire. The victim becomes the oppressor. It was great fun!

TWIN MIRRORS

Aims: Seeing what we look at, spontaneity, concentration, interaction, communication
Average length: 20 minutes
Materials and preparation: None

■ Action and procedure

Split the group into pairs. Tell everybody that the object of this game is to do nothing but face your partner and mirror everything that your partner does. The slightest movement (even if it was just a reaction to an itch) must be mirrored by your partner. Both parties are in effect the initiator and the mirror and will be reflecting themselves being reflected. While this game is going on the leader should say to people, "Did you initiate that movement? Or did you reflect what you saw?", keeping participants aware of the fact that they are only a mirror.

■ Variation

Take it in turns to be a mirror and an initiator.

■ Closure

At the end the leader should ask everyone how this game made them feel and share these experiences with the group verbally or non-verbally.

EXCALIBUR

Aims: Body skills, use of imagination, warm-up
Average length: 40 minutes
Materials and preparation: None

■ Action and procedure

Before the game starts the leader must privately decide on a formula. Ask the group to imagine a rock with a sword sticking out of it in the middle of the room. The object of this game is to get the sword out of the rock. Ask each person in turn to show how they would attempt to get the sword out. Inform them that they may use any method they want, including using others in the group to help. They must mime their attempt, showing all the effort they are expending. They will know if they are successful as they will hear a loud bang. The group leader will know the key to the puzzle and if anyone finds the right key then the group leader should shout "bang!" The key could be anything such as 'a person who uses the whole group to help pull the sword out' or 'a person that runs round the sword three times, shouts a magic word and pulls the sword with their teeth' — whatever the group leader decides.

■ Closure

If no-one retrieves the sword, the group leader should draw the game to a close at an appropriate point and talk to the group about how the game made them feel.

WHICH WORD WITCH?

Aims: Imagination, group interaction, communication, sharing, fun
Average length: 60 minutes
Materials and preparation: Pens and paper

■ Action and procedure

Get the group into a circle. The leader says: "I am the word witch and am taking away all your words actually, you can keep five words as I'm in a good mood." Get each participant to write down their five words and then find a partner. Each pair may now share their words (giving them a total vocabulary of ten words). Get pairs to 'socialize' with each other using their shared words only. Encourage the group to mix as if at a party. After participants have talked to five or six people (and shared words) get everyone to write a short poem or story with their words.

■ Closure

Bring the group back into a circle, share poems and stories and how it felt to communicate with a limited vocabulary. What else did people use to communicate with each other?

EXPLOSION TIG

Aims: Boundary setting, improvisation, high energy, fun
Average length: 20 minutes
Materials and preparation: None

■ Action and procedure

This is similar to the children's game 'tig' where, if you are touched by the person who is 'it', you become 'it'. Split the group into two. Establish a small playing area (say 7 by 7 metres [23 by 23 feet] for 15 players). The first half of the group forms the boundary and the other half plays. The leader shouts, "Last one in the middle is it." This is a game of tig within the set boundaries. After a few minutes of playing, when the energy levels are high, the leader adds another rule: when tagged, a player must take a few seconds to explode — they may explode however they wish. After several minutes of playing, swap the groups over.

■ Variation

Make the playing area smaller. Get participants to explode in ever-increasing spirals.

■ Closure

At the end of the exercise, ask the group how the exercise made them feel.

IT'S NOT MY PARTY

Aims: Trust, self-disclosure, interaction, communication, improvisation, identifying attitudes
Average length: 30 minutes
Materials and preparation: None

■ Action and procedure

Ask participants to become one of their parents and invite them all to a party. Without leaving the space get everyone to socialize with the other guests, talking about their children. Make sure people listen as well as talk. After a few minutes bring the group into a circle and do a round of 'I discovered …'

■ Variation

Rather than a parent become a bureaucrat, an official or a participant's teacher or boss.

■ Closure

Share and explore discoveries.

POLICEMAN

Aims: Concentration, use of imagination, creativity, communication
Average length: 15 minutes
Materials and preparation: Written instructions on a sheet of paper

■ Action and procedure

First of all choose a policeman. Give him the written instructions. The policeman stands in the middle and reads to the group: "Starting now, you must not answer when I speak to you; the person on your left must answer for you. You must not nod or smile or respond to me or anyone else in any way. If you do then you will be out. If you are out, you must slowly walk around the circle muttering. As people get out they will link up with the others who are out by walking behind them muttering a 'common mutter'. Do you understand?" Some people invariably answer (and they will be out). The policeman starts again, asking each person questions and putting them out if they answer. The conga-like mutter will be circling the group, ever increasing in size and volume. The muttering could take the form of barracking, lost souls, cheerleaders or whatever the first one out chooses — the rest follow in a common mutter.

■ Closure

People share how they feel.

SILENCE IS GOLDEN

Aims: Sensory awareness, self-validation, trust, body skills, voice skills, improvisation
Average length: 10 minutes
Materials and preparation: Silence

■ Action and procedure

Ask everyone in the group to find a space as far away from anyone else in the room as they can and to either sit or lie down on the floor with their eyes closed. When this has been achieved, ask everyone for a complete golden silence and no contact with any other group member. Let this silence fill the room for a minute or two and then go on to explain that, as you walk around the room, you will touch people on the shoulder. Immediately someone is touched they must leap up with their own choice of exclamation and literally tear the silence in two (for example, with a scream). Wherever they land they must resume their silent pose. It is important to wait for calm before touching the next shoulder.

■ Variation

Do not wait for calm before touching the next shoulder, so that it becomes almost a 'Mexican scream'.

■ Closure

At the end of the exercise, ask everyone how they feel and to share this with the group verbally or non-verbally.

STICKY PAPER

Aims: Use of imagination, group interaction, contact
Average length: 20 minutes
Materials and preparation: One sheet of paper for each group member

■ Action and procedure

One person is put in the centre of a circle. The others touch them or one another, but with a sheet of paper between the touching parts of the bodies. When this has been achieved the person in the centre begins to move and the whole group must move with them and the pieces of paper must stay where they are, without being dropped. Continue this as long as people are having fun.

■ Closure

Talk with the group about the game. How do they feel? Was it as difficult as they thought it would be?

THE GAME OF MACHINES

Aims: Spontaneity, getting in touch with what we can see and hear, group interaction, body skills, movement and voice skills
Average length: 30 minutes
Materials and preparation: None

■ Action and procedure

The group forms a circle and sits. One person is asked to go into the centre and imagine they are part of a complicated mechanical machine. They start making a movement with their body and vocalizing a sound to go with it. Everyone else watches and listens. One by one people are asked to add themselves to the machine, becoming another part of it, until eventually the whole group has made a synchronized, complex machine. When the whole machine is assembled, the group leader asks the person who began to start going faster, the whole group should follow at the same pace with their integrated rhythms until the machine is about to explode, at which point it should start to slow down, until it eventually stops.

■ Variation

Give the machine a name before you start.

■ Closure

At the end of the exercise, ask everyone how this game made them feel and share these experiences with the group verbally or non-verbally.

SAVE ME

Aims: Movement, concentration, group interaction
Average length: 10 minutes
Materials and preparation: None

■ Action and procedure

Everyone is asked to find a point in the room as far away from anyone else as possible. Without telling anyone who it is, everyone is asked to pick someone in the room who is a demon. Each person can move now, but the object of the game is to stay as far as possible from the person each has chosen as their demon. After a while the group leader asks everyone to pick another person who is the demon slayer. Again no one should say or indicate who their demon slayer is. The group is asked to move around the space again, this time keeping their demon slayer *between* them and their demon. As things get more frantic the group leader should start a countdown, saying to the group, "When I reach zero everyone should freeze where they are."

■ Closure

See who has succeeded in evading their demon. Talk with the group about this game and how they feel.

PASS THE CLAP

Aims: Concentration, group interaction, integration of senses
Average length: 20 minutes
Materials and preparation: None

■ Action and procedure

Part 1

Ask the group to form a circle. The group leader should be part of the circle and start the clap off. The group is told that it is going to pass round claps to the person on their immediate left and then they will do the same to their right. It is important how these claps are given and received: you look to your left and when that person turns and looks you in the eye (everyone keeping their feet firmly pointing forward) you clap in front of them; they take that clap by clapping once immediately while still looking at you and then they turn to the person on their left and the whole procedure starts again as they wait for that person to look them in the eye and pass them the clap.

Part 2

The clap continues around the circle. After a while the clap will seem to glide around the circle like a Mexican wave. When a good rhythm has been achieved, start increasing the speed of the clap journey around the circle. See how fast you can send the clap round.

■ Variations

Send round multiple claps. Send claps round in both directions (in this variation it is important to note that for best results people should concentrate on those next to them, rather than watch the claps being passed round).

■ Closure

At the end of the exercise, ask everyone how they feel.

THE EMBASSY BALL

Aims: Use of imagination, creativity, improvisation, creation of characters, group interaction, exploration of desires
Average length: 60 minutes
Materials and preparation: None
Caution: Not suitable for all groups

■ Action and procedure

Part 1

Everyone is asked to pick a character that they will play during this game. These characters can be anybody: a famous actor, a musician, a judge, a lawyer, a parent, and so on. One person is invited to play a waiter and another the host (who we will call the Sultan) to whose residence all these characters will be invited for a party. The group gathers at one end of the space. The Sultan leaves the others and announces that they are holding a party and everyone is invited. As each guest is announced, they join the Sultan. When everyone is mingling (as their characters and in their best clothes) the waiter goes round with a tray of drinks which they offer to each of the guests. The group leader should announce that, unbeknown to the guests or the Sultan, the waiter is a revolutionary and has spiked the drink with a hallucinogenic drug.

Part 2

As this first drink goes round, everyone starts to behave strangely. After a little while the waiter takes round a second set of drinks. These drinks contain more of the drug and the guests start to reveal more of themselves, as all their inhibitions have gone; they really open up as they cease to be able to retain their masks of respectability. A third round of drinks is now brought round by the waiter. This again is spiked with more of the same drug. The guests now start to behave very strangely and share their characters' less inhibited selves with each other more intimately. For example, if someone was playing the part of the prime minister, they might make up a scandal in Parliament. Eventually, the waiter brings round a fourth round of drinks which contains an antidote to the drug and all the guests return to their socially acceptable selves.

■ Variations

Instead of a party it could be a board of directors' meeting or a school governors' meeting.

■ Closure

The group leader should decide when to call a halt to the game, bring all the participants into a circle and talk to them about how this game made them feel. Participants talk about their characters and the changes that occurred in them. Does this tell us anything about ourselves?

HELLO

Aims: Warm-up, introductions, communication, group interaction
Average length: 10 minutes
Materials and preparation: None

■ Action and procedure

Everyone is asked to say "Hello, how are you?" to all the other group members. Before anyone can say this, they must be shaking hands with the person they are speaking to. Before anyone can disengage from a handshake they must start up a handshake with someone else; that is, they must always have at least one hand shaking hands with someone. When each has greeted all, the group leader can extend the game by asking for another phrase to be exchanged in a similar manner, such as "Thank you".

■ Variation

This game can also be used as a closure, with group members saying "Goodbye" to each other.

■ Closure

At an appropriate time, bring the game to an end and ask people how they feel.

Images in action

Images are an excellent means of exploration within the group. Image work is non-threatening and people do not feel 'put-on-the-spot'. Through image work we can look at ways in which transformations are possible within any situation. These transformations can be viewed step-by-step.

When using images, people do not have the same feelings of discomfort that they often feel when they have to talk or 'perform' in front of a group. People are not exposed in a way that is threatening.

Just as a child can see things before it knows what they are called we can say that an image comes before words. We can therefore recognize an image without ever having to verbalize it. We could, for example, hold out our hand, as if we were going to shake someone else's hand, and freeze. If we had not explained what we were doing, it is possible that people would offer different interpretations such as "They are going to slap someone", or "Gimme' five", "Hands up", "He's reaching for help" or "He's spraying his crops", and so on.

If people have difficulties with words then image work is an excellent medium to use.

We can place ourselves in relation to an image; in fact we can put ourselves in it — so we can create an image and then put ourselves inside it. We can also put someone else in our image and so observe what we look like to others.

Every image embodies a way of seeing. Each creator of an image will be different and no two images will ever be exactly the same. An image will say something different to everybody: each part of it will mean something to us, as will the whole. So an image speaks to us as words never can. We can lose ourselves within an image, where words might have been a barrier. Images therefore open up alternative paths for us to use.

An image a day keeps the doctor away!

CHANGE THE IMAGE

Aims: To introduce the use of images, social development, sharing, taking and losing, creativity, non-vocal communication (NVC)
Average length: 25 minutes
Materials and preparation: Enough chairs for half the group to have one each

■ Action and procedure

Part 1

Ask the group to get into pairs and to name themselves A and B. A starts by freezing into an image of his/her choice, an image of anything they like — it does not have to mean anything. B looks at this frozen image for a couple of seconds and then puts him/herself into the image with an image of his/her own. (So B has complemented the image; B has not moved A but has managed to change A's image by putting him/herself in it.) This newly created image is held for a couple of seconds and then A comes out of the image, leaving B frozen in the chosen position. A looks at the image for a couple of seconds and then puts him/herself back in the image with a different image of his/her own. Again this newly created image is held for a couple of seconds and then B comes out of the image, leaving A frozen in the chosen position. B looks at the image of A and then goes back in again with another image — and so it goes on.

Part 2

This evolving image should be allowed to go on for some minutes, allowing people to experiment and to develop a rapport with each other. After a while each pair is offered the use of a chair as a prop to use in their images. The group leader should stress that they do not have to use the chair if they do not want to. The game now uses the same format as before, except that now each person can bring the chair into the image to represent anything they like. The chair can be removed and repositioned on each successive move (unless to do so would cause injury, as when moving it if someone is standing on it).

■ Closure

The group leader should decide when it is appropriate to call an end to this game. Talk to the group about how this game made them feel. Did people use the chair? Was it more or less difficult using the chair? Did stories evolve? How did it feel when their image was changed? How did it feel to create a new image? What kinds of images were created?

BASIC SCULPT

Aims: Group interaction, creativity, self-revelation
Average length: 60 minutes
Materials and preparation: None

■ Action and procedure

Part 1

Ask the group to form a circle and ask for one volunteer to become a sculptor. Tell the sculptor that they can choose up to three people from the group that are going to be their models. Say to the sculptor that they can now build or mould an image of their choice with their three subjects. The subjects are placed in the centre of the circle and the sculptor bends, turns, joins, pulls and pushes them into an image of the sculptor's choice. The subjects act like pieces of clay; they cannot talk or move by themselves; whatever position the sculptor puts them in they should freeze. While the sculptor is sculpting, remind them that they should put in as much detail as they can. When the sculptor has finished tell them to walk around their image a few times to see that it is just how they want it. If it is then ask them to place themselves in relation to the model so that they become part of the image themselves (there should have been no analysing of the image up to this point — the sculptor should not verbalize the image at all).

Part 2

Invite the audience (the remaining participants) to walk around the image and to look at every part of it. What do they see? What is the image telling us? What do they feel it represents? When everyone in the audience has had a say, ask someone to take the place of the sculptor, so that the latter can have a look at the total image. Ask the sculptor what they thought about participants' verbalizing of the image (the sculptor does not have to say what it meant to them). Thank the models and try a new image with a different volunteer.

■ Closure

At the end, talk to the group about the images. What did people say about the images? What kinds of feelings were represented? How did people feel when they saw themselves in the image? What were the range of feelings represented in the images? How did this exercise make people feel?

GROUP BODY SCULPT

Aims: Group transaction, sensitivity, creativity
Average length: 60 minutes
Materials and preparation: None

■ Action and procedure

Part 1

Ask the group to propose a theme to work on (such as 'family', 'death', 'money', 'stress', 'love'). Ask a volunteer to pick people from the group and create a picture of the proposed theme. The group leader should then consult the group to see if they agree with the picture. If they do, leave it. If they do not then someone may build another image, or just 'tinker at the edges'. If the whole group finds an acceptable image, this is called the *ideal*.

Part 2

What is ideal for one person is not necessarily so for another and the group may have to set up a series of images to represent everyone's view. For example, if the topic of the family is chosen, people may have different ideas of what a family is — a one-parent family, a family from another country, a heterosexual family, a lesbian family, a two-parent family and so on.

■ Closure

Is it possible to come up with an image of the perfect family? What is the perfect family? Talk about the images with the group. What did they see? What did they like? What did they dislike?

TRANSFORMING OPPRESSION

Aims: Group transaction, sensitivity, creativity, dealing with change, exploring oppression
Average length: 90 minutes
Materials and preparation: None

■ Action and procedure

Part 1

Ask a volunteer to pick people from the group and to put them into an image of an oppressive situation. When this is done, the group leader should consult the group to see if they can see elements of oppression in the image. If they do, leave it; if they do not then someone may take it to pieces and rebuild another image of oppression, or they may just tinker at the edges if it is nearly right. If an image is found that the whole group finds acceptable, use it. What is oppressive for one person is not necessarily so for another and the group may have to set up a series of images to represent everyone's view.

Part 2

Once there is an image (or a series of images) of oppression that everyone agrees with, ask the group to construct the 'ideal' image, where all the oppression has been taken out and all the characters in the image have reached a state of perfect equilibrium with each other. Once this is done, place the two images side by side. What do we see? What changes have occurred? Ask people in turn to show what characters might have done to get from being oppressed to not being oppressed.

■ Closure

How do the images feel? Are these real solutions or could they not happen in real life? Why? Everyone shares their feelings with the group.

MY FAMILY

Aims: Self-disclosure, creativity, imagination, distancing, sharing
Average length: 60 minutes
Materials and preparation: None

■ Action and procedure

Ask people to work in groups of five. Each person in each group should create two images, using their group members as models. The first image should be of 'my family' and the second image of 'my ideal family'. Each person works in turn so that after a period of time each group has 10 images. These images no longer belong to the individual — they belong to the group. Give the groups 10 minutes to remember or rehearse each of the images and then ask each group, one by one, to show the whole group their 10 images.

■ Closure

How many different types of family were portrayed? Was every family recognized? What roles did people have in these families? Were the ideals a possible reality? Why was the ideal different from the actual? Ask the group how this exercise made them feel.

IMAGE OF THE GROUP

Aims: Tackling group difficulties, creativity, imagining, sharing
Average length: 60 minutes
Materials and preparation: None

■ Action and procedure

Part 1

This exercise can be used at any time but is particularly useful when the group leader feels that the group itself is not working as well as it could. It is also a good way of seeing how each participant sees the group as a whole. Sometimes people may not want to participate in a group, may just want to prevaricate or just feel plain stubborn. It is at times like this that the group may not be able to build one image that everyone is happy with or that everyone has made a contribution to.

The group leader should invite volunteers to build an image of the group, continually consulting the group on progress made, adding or taking away elements that are non-essential.

Part 2

Eventually an image is created and the group leader reminds everyone that they are part of the image. Even those people who refused to participate are part of the overall image because they are taking roles of people who are refusing to participate. So within the room you will have one giant image with a nucleus of people on the inside and people on the outside who are refusing to participate or maybe are just 'happy watching'. Now tell those people who are happy with their positions in the nucleus to stay there and those that are unhappy about their positions in the nucleus to go and sit down. The group leader should also tell those that are not participating or are just watching that, if they feel uncomfortable with their positions, they may either join the nucleus or go and sit down. After all these movements have been made the group leader asks the participants to come out of the image and to go back in wherever they want (that is, not in a position that has been imposed on them). This final image should show whether the group is able to work together harmoniously, what transformations may be needed to help and what hidden grievances people may be holding.

■ Closure

Talk to the group about these images. How did they make them feel? Are divisions too great?

VOLLEYBALL

Aims: Movement, group interaction, warm-up, fun
Average length: 20 minutes
Materials and preparation: None

■ Action and procedure

Split the group up into two teams, with one person acting as referee. The group must now play a game of volleyball, acting as if there were a ball and a net. The imaginary movements of the ball must correspond closely to the actions of the participants. The referee's decision is final.

■ Variation

Football, cricket (or any ball game).

■ Closure

At the end of the game, talk to the group about how this game made them feel.

IMAGE OF THE OBJECT

Aims: To discover relationships, to stimulate imagination, group transaction, projection
Average length: 30 minutes
Materials and preparation: Each participant has been asked to bring in five objects, objects that they have used in their lives.

■ Action and procedure

The group is invited to place their objects anywhere in the space that they like. When all the objects have been positioned, the group analyses the relationship each object has with any other. Have any families of objects been found? Are there any connections between different groups of objects? Why have things been placed where they are? What do the objects mean to us, what meaning have we projected onto them?

■ Closure

Talk with the group about how this exercise made them feel.

CHANGE THE IMAGE OF THE OBJECT

Aims: To stimulate imagination, projection, change, creativity, perception
Average length: 20 minutes
Materials and preparation: Each participant has been asked to bring in two objects, objects that they have used in their lives.

■ Action and procedure

Each participant is given someone else's object and has to show what else it could be apart from what it is. Remember, anything can become anything (see the game, 'What's in a bottle?', p 97). For example, "This is not a shoe, it is an ear-ring" (hang the shoe from the ear). Through images (no talking) participants, in turn, should show what these objects could have been used for.

■ Closure

When everyone has had a go, talk to the group about how this game made them feel.

TEN QUESTIONS

Aims: Observation, use of imagination, confidence building, fun
Average length: Up to 5 minutes each
Materials and preparation: None

■ Action and procedure

One person is asked to leave the space while the others create an image of someone working (it can be realistic, symbolic or whatever else they may choose). The person is invited back into the room and has to try and guess the nature of the occupation depicted by the image. No talking is allowed. This person is allowed 10 attempts to put themselves in the image, as though they were part of the workforce, with a ritualized movement or gesture. If they are right they are given hearty applause, if wrong they are given boos and if on the right track they are given applause mixed in with a bit of heckling. If after 10 attempts they have not managed to guess the occupation, the image has won. Someone else leaves the room and another image is created. This procedure is repeated until everyone who wants a go has had a go.

■ Closure

At the end, talk with the group about how this game made them feel.

Scenes in action

Using theatre techniques we can explore an endless variety of subjects. Creating a scene, we can present a topic from many points of view. Groups can participate in real time and unreal time, in reality and in fantasy. Everyone is included, even the audience, sharing a multitude of solutions and providing a safe space that allows us to go as far as we are prepared to go — and a bit further.

The games and exercises which follow should not be attempted before the group is thoroughly warmed up and has played some games from 'The senses in action' and 'Images in action'. This is essential in getting the best out of a session. An excellent way to get the group in the mood is to run some of the image exercises first.

I have borrowed ideas from many branches of action methods, including dramatherapy, psychodrama, forum theatre and theatre in education. I am not a therapist but I believe that theatre is a very therapeutic medium, so I am going to call this combination of techniques 'theatretherapy'.

The reader may be surprised that I have used some Shakespeare. Most of us have had poor experiences of Shakespeare at school and tend to think his writing is too complicated or obscure. However, we need to remember that Shakespeare's themes are everybody's themes: love, jealousy, oppression, depression, madness, and so on. He writes with extraordinary understanding of families and relationships. It is these universal themes that I make use of.

FORUM THEATRE MODEL

Aims: To help people understand what is meant by forum theatre
Average length: Over an hour
Materials and preparation: Warm up

■ **Action and procedure**

This is *not* another game or exercise, but a report of a forum theatre session run with a group of probation clients and officers. It is put in here for the benefit of the first-time user of forum theatre, as a guide to what can happen or what possibilities there are. Bear in mind that there are many different forms of forum theatre, run all over the world, and slight adaptations work better for some groups' needs than they do for others. Also remember that there is no right or wrong way: you do it the way that best suits your group.

Working with this probation group, the topic of bereavement was chosen. Several of the participants had had recent deaths in the family and had found this difficult to cope with. They set up a scene where an only son's mother dies from a long, painful illness. He is not ready for the death and neither is his father.

First action

A young man, Terry, is sitting at home in his room, doing nothing. The phone rings; he ignores it. The front door bell rings; he ignores it. He is staring blankly at his bedroom wall.

Second action

Terry's father comes home and invites him down to the pub. Terry declines. An argument ensues, with his father saying things like "You can't mourn your mother forever; snap out of it."

Third action

Terry's friends are talking about him. "He won't come out and every time you ask if he's all right he bites your head off." They try to talk to him, but he just sits glumly.

The forum

Here we see Terry consumed by grief that he will not let out. He will not let anyone help him and he blames his father for the death of his mother. His father, it seems, does not care about him or his mother. His father is also in a state of denial and has not cried yet over the death of his wife.

The second time the piece was performed by some of the group members to the rest of the group, the audience were invited to stop the action whenever they thought they could offer an alternative course. In the first action, the scene was stopped repeatedly when the phone was ringing. Several audience members took it in turn to answer the phone and talk to an imaginary person on the other end who, in most cases, was offering help. Then a few people started playing the part of the 'imaginary person on the other end'. On these occasions Terry was invited out to parties, day trips and a 'rave'. None of these seemed to have much effect on Terry's happiness. One of the audience members started to talk about her own difficulties, dealing with her feelings about her brother being in hospital. Terry opened up a little about himself during this conversation; he was seeing that such things did not just happen to him. Just after that intervention, an audience member stopped the action, took the place of Terry, listened to the phone ringing for a few seconds and then broke down and cried and cried and cried.

At this point we let the forum carry on into the second action, with the father coming home. Another member of the audience, playing the part of the father, came into the room of the crying Terry and put her arms around him and hugged him tight. That was a very emotional scene and ended with cheers and tears from the audience. After a brief break the original actors were back, performing the third action.

Most of the stops were similar to those made earlier, getting Terry to interact with his friends. The audience member who had played Terry's father during an earlier intervention stopped the scene again and this time took over the role of Terry. She grabbed her three friends and started shouting at them. They were shocked and offended. She then apologized and started talking about being mixed up over her mother's death; there was so much she had not told her mother and now it was too late. Then she asked if they minded her telling them. They all shook their heads, with mutters of "Of course not". They were there for her. There were several further interventions before the end of the session: one showing Terry finding solace in the church; another with Terry ignoring the pain and 'carrying on with life'; Terry giving up everything and starting life anew somewhere else; Terry entering bereavement counselling. All of the interventions showed a possible path that Terry could take at *that moment* in his life. No-one was telling Terry what he should do: they were saying, "Have you thought about doing it like this?" That is what happens in a forum theatre session — we all share our strategies for life, for difficult situations, and in particular we share the way we deal with oppressive situations, whatever form they take.

In forum theatre we have entered a new space, a safe space. Within this safe space we can experiment. If we like some of the results of our experimentation then we can use them in our lives, in reality, if we want to.

FORUM THEATRE 1

Aims: Exploration, improvisation, group transaction
Average length: 60 minutes (minimum)
Materials and preparation: Group warm-up

■ Action and procedure

Part 1

Decide on a topic that the group wishes to explore (such as sexism, racism, bullying, bereavement and so on). Split the group into audience (65 per cent) and actors (35 per cent). The actors are going to improvise a very short scene on the chosen topic to the audience. Give the actors five minutes to talk about the chosen topic and who is going to play what in the scene (if, for example, the subject of bullying was chosen, the actors would have to show somebody being bullied in some way). After five minutes ask the actors to come and perform their scene. It should be between two and three minutes long. When the scene is finished, ask the audience to comment on the content of the piece (not the acting). Who was being bullied? Why? What could they have done? What would you have done?

Part 2

After a minute of discussion, ask the actors to replay the scene. This time the audience have a chance to alter the destiny of the characters in the play. They are told that, whenever they see a chance for the person being picked on to make their situation better, they should shout "Stop" and the actors will freeze in their positions. The person who shouted is then coaxed out of their seat into the playing area. They are asked to show what they would have done in that particular situation. So they take the place of the actor who was being picked on in the performance and act out what they would have done. The other actors have to improvise around this new actor. (They should be thinking, does this character's new actions make any difference to my character? If they do, then I must change, as I would in real life.) Once the new way has been tried, *other people are invited to show what they would do.* Do this as many times (and with as many interventions) as is required. Remember that there are no *better* ways, there are just *different* ways. What is right for one person is not necessarily right for another. It is important that the actors stay true to their characters and do not make it too easy for the interventionist.

■ Closure

At the end of the session talk to the group about how this exercise made them feel. What did they see? How many different solutions were there? Why did X work and why did Y not work so well? Can we use what we have discovered in real life? Why?

FORUM THEATRE 2

Aims: Exploration, improvisation, group transaction
Average length: 120 minutes (minimum)
Materials and preparation: The group should be thoroughly warmed up

■ Action and procedure

Part 1

Decide on two topics that the group wishes to explore (they should be issues that are important to the group). Split the group in half, with each group having one of the topics. Both groups should now go and devise a scene around their topic. They should also be given time to rehearse the scene. It is recommended that 30 to 60 minutes be given for this activity. After rehearsal, the two groups take turns to perform their pieces. When both performances have been watched, the group (as a whole) should spend some time discussing what they saw. Have the issues been performed correctly? Did characters behave as they might in real life? What kinds of oppression have we seen portrayed? Is it possible for the characters to make their lives more liveable?

Part 2

After discussion and a break (tea anyone?) get the groups to spend another 30 minutes refining their pieces, taking account of what has been raised in the discussion. The groups are now ready for the forum. As seen in 'Forum theatre 1' the forum is like a battle between the actors and the audience. The audience want to help anyone they see oppressed in the scene and the actors do not want to make it too easy for them to change (staying true to their characters).

The groups take turns, once again. This time the first group starts their scene and the audience are invited to stop the play whenever they see a character in some kind of difficulty. The person who stopped the play is encouraged to take the place of the actor who was in difficulty and show a possible way out. The group leader should encourage all kinds of interventions: "Try anything — see if it works." All kinds of bizarre attempts might reveal a way to overcome an oppression that had previously been hidden. When taking over an actor's role the interventionist should tell the other actors where to restart the play. As this new person will be going away from the script, the actors must improvise around the changes.

Part 3

It is important that the actors stay true to their characters and do not make it too easy for the interventionist. Having said this, they should also allow for changes in their characters if what the interventionist does would have (in real life) changed their character's actions. After each intervention, the group leader should check with the audience whether they thought characters played as they would have done if it had been real life. Encourage other audience members to show different ways of overcoming the difficulty. Repeat this process until the end of the scene. Now the groups swap over and the forum process is repeated once again.

This exercise is very flexible indeed. The length of the exercise, for example, could be anything from three hours in a single day's workshop to three weeks (or even longer) in a long-running workshop. Find out how the group feels at the end of each session. Are everyone's views being represented? Are the solutions found real solutions; that is, can they be transferred to reality? If people manage to overcome difficulties in a forum theatre setting then they could also overcome them if the same situation arises in reality. In effect the group are sharing their ideas with one another through the language of theatre.

■ Closure

Actors should symbolically leave their characters and return to themselves. There should be a big group hug, followed by sharing feelings.

SHAKESPEARE 1

Aims: Expanding awareness of the body, development of imagination
Average length: 15 minutes
Materials and preparation: Possibly some pictures of Elizabethan costumes for the group to look at.

■ Action and procedure

Invite the group to walk as if they are wearing a hat with a very large feather in it, boots with tops turned over, large padded breeches and dresses with hoops in them.

Let the group develop stylized movements and gestures and then interact with each other.

■ Closure

Compare variations in body feelings. Did the walk or the gesture give any insight into the characters?

SHAKESPEARE 2

Aims: Learning new languages
Average length: 25 minutes
Materials and preparation: A copy for each person of a well-known Shakespearian sonnet.

■ Action and procedure

Give people time to read through the sonnet (for people who cannot read, the group leader should read it to them). Go round the group with participants reading one line each.

Invite people to read the sonnet to a partner and then to listen while the partner reads it to them.

■ Closure

Share ideas about the language of love and people's attitudes to Shakespeare.

SHAKESPEARE 3

Aims: Exploring families, improvisation
Average length: 30 minutes (minimum)
Materials and preparation: The group should be warmed up

■ Action and procedure

Instead of exploring their own families, people can feel safe exploring a Shakespearian family, such as King Lear and his daughters. If the group do not know the play, the group leader can read them the story. Then the group can choose a theme from the story and improvise it and then go back to the script and compare, or read the story in Lamb's *Tales from Shakespeare*.

■ Closure

Talk about the different kinds of family. Are our own families similar? Help everyone to share their feelings with the group.

USING SHAKESPEARE

Aims: Widening perception, insight, change, experimentation, understanding Shakespeare
Average length: 60 minutes (minimum)
Materials and preparation: The group should be warmed up vocally and physically. They will have played some drama games. They will need a Shakespearian text to work with.

■ Action and procedure

Part 1

The group leader will first of all have to have a feel for the 'theme' that is running through the group. Why is the group meeting? The group leader should then pick a play text from Shakespeare that contains issues the group are dealing with. For example, the interpretations of *Macbeth* are numerous. Many people talk of a representation of evil, a battle between the souls of Macbeth and his wife. In contrast, we see the 'good' of Duncan and Malcolm. So is the play about heaven and hell? About good and evil? One continuous theme running through the play is the question of honour. Honour can bring a sense of self-worth, which can also give us ideas of 'our duties within society'. Whatever our interpretation of the play, it could be a good text to use when exploring the subject of male/female relationships.

Part 2

If we have a theme of male/female relationships running through the group, how is the play going to help us explore this subject without making group members feel exposed? Remember that we will be using the dramatic distance; the play will contain everyone's story, everyone will be able to look at what is appropriate to their lives.

If it is not possible for the group to have previously seen the play then the group leader should give as detailed a summary as possible of the play to the group, reading out certain sections, or getting group members to read certain roles. The group are then ready to embark on their experimentation.

Take a few lines from the play. If the theme is male/female relationships, for example, these lines might be chosen: 'Pr'ythee, peace. I dare do all that may become a man; who dares do more, is none' (I, vii, 45) . Here we have Macbeth plotting with Lady Macbeth. Split the group up into pairs and get each pair to do repeated improvisations around the chosen lines. Encourage them to immerse themselves in the two characters and their complex relationship.

Part 3

Exploring these improvisations will allow people to take their own journey through the recognition of what is in themselves. Each of the pairs will have different struggles and each will have to use individual skills in this joint endeavour.

■ Closure

The group leader should call a halt at an appropriate moment and bring everyone together to derole. Everyone should also feel distanced from any of the stories that have emerged. At this point the group can share 'hot themes' that came out of the improvisations. Why do people embark on relationships? Why do people feel pressured into doing things they do not want? What makes relationships work? What is love? These could be some of the questions raised, along with many more. Make sure that equal weight is given to everybody's feelings.

(**NB** The group does not have to stay with Shakespeare. There are many myths and stories that could replace or complement Shakespeare and in fact could be used to follow up issues raised in the improvisations.)

REVELATIONS

Aims: Exploring relationships, improvisation, characterization, dealing with change
Average length: 100 minutes (minimum)
Materials and preparation: The group should be thoroughly warmed up.

■ Action and procedure

Part 1

The group decides on a type of relationship to explore (this relationship can be anything such as parent and child, boyfriend and girlfriend, teacher and student, individual and official, doctor and patient). The group leader should ask everyone to find a partner and tell them to decide who is playing what, where they would usually meet and how old they are.

Simultaneously, each pair meets and begins an improvisation on where their characters meet, how they greet each other and what they might normally say. Give them a few minutes to get to know their characters and then bring them all into a circle. Tell everybody to remember how and where they met and what was said.

Part 2

Ask the first couple to go into the centre of the circle and show everybody where and how they met. After a few minutes the group leader should say, "One of you make a revelation of great importance that has a potential to change your relationship." (For example, "I'm pregnant" or "I've got a new job" or "I'm having an affair with your wife" or "I'm going away".) The other person should react in the way they feel their character would react in real life. After a few more minutes the group leader should tell the other one to make an important revelation, at which their partner should react in the way they feel their character would. How is their relationship now? Next, the group leader should tell one of them that they have to leave. The couple should improvise their parting. Will they ever see each other again? The group leader should thank the couple and ask them to sit down. Each pair in turn is asked up and should follow the same procedure as the first.

How did this game make people feel? What was the range of

revelations and how did people react? Why did people react in certain ways? How many stereotypes did we see?

Part 3

Ask the group now to pick several of the improvisations to be repeated. They should try to pick ones that were highly charged. Take the first improvisation up to the point of the reaction to the first revelation and then shout "Stop!" Ask if any of the group members would like to show a possible different reaction. Replay the scene with as many different reactions as people want to offer, then do the same thing with the second revelation and then the parting. Repeat with several more chosen improvisations.

■ Closure

Talk with the group about how this made them feel. How many ways of reacting to a situation are there? How did reactions change the relationships?

ROLE REVERSAL

Aims: Self-exploration, trust, communication
Average length: 40 minutes
Materials and preparation: The group should be thoroughly warmed up.

■ Action and procedure

Ask everyone to find a partner (someone they are happy sharing something with), to name themselves A or B and to sit down together as far away from anyone else as possible. A should tell B a story of a difficult relationship they have with someone in their lives. A talks about a typical place where they would have to deal with this person and what is said and done in the meetings that they have. After a few minutes ask them to improvise a typical encounter, with A playing themselves and B playing the person that A talked about. After a few more minutes they should reverse roles: B should play A, and A should play the character of the person they had the difficulty with. When a few more minutes have passed, ask them to revert to their original roles and start the improvisation again. Have people changed?

■ Closure

Bring the group back together and talk to them about how they feel. What was it like watching themselves? Did people modify their behaviour?

RITUAL 1

Aims: Movement, creativity, group interaction, preparation for 'Ritual 2'
Average length: 30 minutes
Materials and preparation: The group should be warmed up.

■ Action and procedure

The group should pick a topic to ritualize (for example, celebrations). It can be about anything, but must be one that the whole group agrees upon. Each person invents a rhythm and sound giving their interpretation of the chosen topic. It does not have to be a naturalistic interpretation; it can take any form, including one which shows people's feelings about the topic. Each person now has their personal ritual. People in turn perform each other's rituals.

■ Closure

Talk about the various rituals. What were the different interpretations like? How does everyone feel?

RITUAL 2

Aims: Movement, use of voice, creativity, group interaction, dealing with change, self-exploration
Average length: 60 minutes (minimum)
Materials and preparation: The group should have done 'Ritual 1'.

■ Action and procedure

Part 1

The group should pick a topic to ritualize (for example, the seasons). It can be about anything, but must be one that the whole group agrees upon. Away from anyone else, each person invents a rhythm and sound giving their interpretation of the chosen topic. It does not have to be a naturalistic interpretation, it can take any form, including one which shows people's feelings about the topic. Now that each person has their own ritual, everybody should mingle around the space, continuing to perform them.

Part 2

The group leader should inform everybody that they can continue on their own, doing their own ritual, or they can join up with others: if they feel an affinity with someone else, they can join up and blend their rituals, so that they end up performing the same one. Both parties have to agree to this blending, which should happen organically, without speech. One party can reject by simply carrying on in another direction. Tell people that groups can be *any* size, so individuals can join groups and groups can join other groups. After each joining a modification in the ritual occurs, with the essence of both rituals being put into the new one. This is done by watching and adapting, slowly, with the parties being drawn together into one.

When the group has become one huge, single ritual, or when no new joinings have occurred for a while, the group leader should draw the game to a close.

■ Closure

Talk about the different interpretations people had. How did people feel when they joined? How did people feel when they did not join or were rejected? What do these images tell us about the chosen topic?

RITUAL 3

Aims: Movement, creativity
Average length: 20 minutes
Materials and preparation: None

■ Action and procedure

The group stands in a circle and, one by one, each person is asked to create a movement of any kind. As each movement is created it is incorporated into all the previous ones. The group thus builds one huge multi-movement structure. The group should attempt to give some meaning to the whole.

■ Closure

Talk with the group about how they feel.

RITUAL 4

Aims: Building a ritual of repair
Average length: 40 minutes
Materials and preparation: The group should be warmed up.

■ Action and procedure

Talk with the group about a topic, such as 'leaving hospital'. After several minutes, ask each person to find a rhythm or a movement that represents, to them, leaving hospital. When everyone has their mini-ritual, ask them to find a partner and to share their rituals with each other.

After a little while ask the pairs to try and incorporate their rituals into one. Eventually, the group leader should bring the group back together and, one by one, the pairs can perform their rituals to the rest of the group.

■ Closure

Were any rituals invented that the group think might help someone who is leaving hospital? Everyone shares with the group how they feel.

THE BAG

Aims: Self-expression, creativity, co-operation
Average length: 40 minutes
Materials and preparation: A bag filled with an assortment of objects. These objects can be anything at all: try to get a variety of colours and textures.

■ Action and procedure

The bag (what the dramatherapist might call a 'Pandora's box of creativity') is placed in front of the group leader who hands out an object to each of the participants. They are asked to go and play with their object in any way they like. After a few moments, tell them that, if they want, they can go up to someone else and try to persuade them to swap objects. If people are happy with their objects then they carry on playing with them and do not have to swap them, but if they have been persuaded to swap then they start to play with their new object. After a few more minutes, ask people to find a partner. Each pair now develops a short scene concerning their two objects. After a little time for rehearsal, ask each pair to perform their scene to the rest of the group.

■ Closure

How did this exercise make people feel? What stories did these objects bring out of us? Did the objects have representations other than that of the object itself?

IMAGE OF THE FAMILY

Aims: Self-exploration, group interaction, improvisation, characterization, change
Average length: 60 minutes (minimum)
Materials and preparation: The group should know each other and be fairly comfortable talking about themselves.

■ Action and procedure

Part 1

Ask the group to form a circle. Ask a volunteer to make an image of their family, using anyone from the circle. They should place these people in relation to each other. They should build this image in the centre of the circle and place the 'family members' as if they were at a typical family gathering. When the image is finished (allow a couple of minutes) ask the volunteer to place themselves in the image 'as themselves'. Everyone should freeze for a few moments while the group leader asks them to remember the image. Thank everyone and tell them they can sit down. Everyone, in turn, follows the same process and builds an image of their family. When all the images have been built and remembered, talk to the group about how they feel and then go on to part 2.

Part 2

Go back to the first image. Everyone takes their position and freezes. The person whose family it is must now give a brief résumé of what their family is like. The group leader then says, "Animate your characters", and the people in the image bring their character alive (as they imagine it from the way they have been placed and from what they have heard). The characters should communicate with each other and the person whose family it is relates to them accordingly. After a few more minutes, the group leader asks the individual if they had the chance to change their family in one way, what it would be. This change is then superimposed upon the animated image. Has the dynamics of the relationships been altered by this one change? Repeat this process with everyone's family.

■ Closure

Talk to the group about how this game made them feel. What did their new families feel like? Will they relate to their families in the same way now? What were the different kinds of family unit?

Follow-up action

Here the reader is taken through the preparation, design, running and evaluation of a workshop session.

With any groupwork it is important for the group leader to ask themselves certain questions, such as those below (written in no order of priority). Answering these questions gives one a good feel for the journey to be embarked upon. It also provides the information needed in preparing the successful workshop.

1 Why am I running this workshop?
2 Have I worked with this group before?
3 What do I hope to achieve?
4 Do I need any help?
5 Will I get all the resources I need?
6 Who will attend this workshop?
7 What are the aims of the workshop?
8 How long is the workshop?
9 Where will I be running the workshop?
10 Which kind of monitoring process should I use?
11 When should I have everything ready?

All groupwork, whether run for a few hours or for a few years, needs a purpose. Having an idea of what we want to achieve allows us to set targets that we can reach. This gives us an idea of moving forward with a group, so that we can get the most out of our valuable time. Our aim may be to have fun or it may be to effect some kind of change or to impart new skills.

Let us take an imaginary journey through the creation of a one-day group session. Writing a plan for the day does not mean that we suddenly commit ourselves to a rigid timetable, but it does give us a safety net if our minds suddenly go blank in the middle of a workshop! I find that having a structure allows me to work freely inside it — each group is different, each group has its own direction or aims. Structures do not mean that one is imposing a way of working but that one is offering the space for exploration and spontaneity to occur. There is no scientific formula that we can use every time. Writing out a plan for the day shows us that we can fit in everything that we want in the time that is available. Go with the flow!

Drawing up the plan

This plan shows one way of introducing a one-day forum theatre workshop.

Aims: To help the participants to get to know each other, to have fun and to provide a vehicle for exploring issues in their lives.
Objective: To show the mechanics of forum theatre
Length: One day (10.00am—6.00 pm)
Size of group: 24
Age range: 16—24

10.00am	Introductions; an ice breaker, such as 'What's in a bottle?' (p 97).
10.10am	Physical exercise session: body and voice warm-up. It is essential to spend 40 minutes on this part. 'The body in action' and 'The voice in action' have many games and exercises to choose from. One suggestion is the use of the 'Tip-to-top' routine (p 19) and Part 1(d) in the voice in action tone and resonance section (p 46). Possibly do some tongue twisters too (pp 50-51).
10.45am	Physical exercise session (sense awareness). I have picked out the following exercises that could be used from earlier sections (you could use any combination): Fill that space (p 102) Deflate me (p 80) Who is the leader? (p 71) Rhythm shoes (p 74) Blind return (p 88)
12.00pm	From 'Games in action', 'Change the president' (p 116) can be played, with a discussion on power relationships afterwards.
12.30pm	Lunch.
1.30pm	From 'Images in action', 'Change the image' (p 142) can be played with the aim of showing the possibilities for change. This will be particularly useful as a preliminary to forum theatre.

2.30pm	From 'Scenes in action', 'Forum theatre 1' (p 159) can be used to explore a chosen topic and to see the possibilities for its application for other exploration.
4.00pm	Tea and coffee break.
4.15pm	Continue 'Forum theatre 1'.
5.15pm	From 'Games in action', 'Back to self' (p 106) can be used to derole.
5.30pm	From 'Games in action', as a closure, use 'Massage circle' (p 107).
5.40pm	Questions and answers (some people need an official slot for these). If you do not know the answer to a question, just say, "I don't know."
5.50pm	Get the evaluation sheets filled in. (There is a sample sheet on pp 191-192.)
6.00pm	Close.

As you can see from this plan, I have picked exercises from different sections, depending on what I want to concentrate on. Each exercise will raise its own issues and can be independent of any of the other exercises. The session will therefore remain flexible enough to go off at any tangent that the group or group leader wants to take.

It is a good idea, especially in a short workshop (when time is all-important), to write down the times when you will be starting each exercise. This will tell you if you are running out of time at any particular point and will allow you to modify in mid-flow.

Whatever you do, do not let the plan stick you in a rut. You do not have to do something for the sake of doing it. If something is not working then talk to the group about it, do something else or explore why it is not working.

It does not take long to evaluate a session and it really will pay dividends for you later (not only will it show how people perceived that workshop, but it will also give you an idea about other needs they have and other follow-up work you could do with them).

Participants are usually quite happy to spend the last five minutes or so filling in a sheet. Remember: if you let them take it away, you most probably will not get it back.

A half-day introductory workshop plan

Aims: For the participants to get to know each other and to have fun
Objective: To break down barriers and remove initial cobwebs
Length: Half a day (9.00am—1.00pm)
Size of group: 24
Age range: 16—24

9.00am	Introductions; an ice breaker, such as 'What's in a bottle?' (p 97).
9.10am	Physical exercise session: body and voice warm-up. It is essential to spend 20 minutes on this part. 'The body in action', and 'The voice in action' have many games and exercises to choose from. One suggestion is the use of the 'Tip-to-top' routine (p 19) and Part 1(d) of the voice in action tone and resonance section (p 46). Possibly do some tongue twisters too (pp 50-51).
9.30am	Choose several games from 'The senses in action' such as 'The Institute of Silly Walks' (p 58) and 'Wink murder' (pp 64-65).
10.30am	Choose several games from 'Games in action', such as 'Minimum surface contact' (p 109) and 'Carnival time' (p 113).
11.30am	'Change the president' (p 116) from 'Games in action'.
12.00pm	Tea and coffee break.
12.15pm	Choose two more games from 'Games in action', such as 'Follow the palm' (p 119) and 'Walking millipede' (p 118).
12.45pm	Questions and Answers (some people need an official slot for these). If you do not know the answer to a question just say "I don't know."
1.00pm	Close.

A one-hour introductory workshop plan

Aims: For the participants to get to know each other and to have fun
Objective: To break down barriers and remove initial cobwebs
Length: One hour (10.00am—11.00am)
Size of group: 24
Age range: 16—24

10.00am	Introductions; an ice breaker, such as 'Fill that space' (p 102).
10.05am	Physical exercise session: body and voice warm-up. It is essential to spend 15 minutes on this part. 'The body in action', and 'The voice in action' have many games and exercises to choose from. One suggestion is to play a quick 'Paper dance' (p 22) and then 'Speech and articulation' (p 48).
10.20am	Choose some complementary games, such as 'Group hum' (p 81) and 'Moving group hum' (p 82).
10.55am	Get the evaluation sheets filled in. (See sample sheet on pp 191-192).
11.00am	Close.

Do not be frightened of experimenting with different games and exercises.

If you are running continuing sessions with the same participants, remember to build on the success of previous sessions. Do not be afraid of repeating games with the same group, especially their *favourite* ones. The group leader should also be aware that many games 'build' into each other.

If you have the time — use it.

APPENDIX

Associated therapies/187
Evaluation/190
Bibliography/193
Alphabetical list of activities/195

ASSOCIATED THERAPIES

Therapy in action

> A lot of therapy is not scientific and is regarded as a matter of luck. Like people hold things called encounter groups. Now this may hurt your feelings. I don't understand encounter groups. They are purely empirical. Nobody really knows what they are doing. Nobody really offers to do anything, actually. But you do get good results. And that applies to a lot of therapy. In other words, roughly speaking, most of the group therapy done in this country — by most I mean 51 per cent — could probably be just as well done by a sophisticated scout master. (Eric Berne, *Beyond Games and Scripts*, p10, Grove Press, New York, 1976)

Not everyone who works with groups of people is necessarily a therapist, but, as Berne illustrates, all kinds of groupwork can be therapeutic. This section looks at some of the different kinds of therapy that have an element of action in them (a selection only). Interested readers could read R. Atkinson *et al*, *Introduction to Psychology*, Harcourt, London, 1985.

'There is an old saying that whenever two Jews meet, if one has a problem, the other automatically becomes a rabbi' (Sheldon Kopp, *If You Meet the Buddha on the Road Kill Him!,* Sheldon Press, London, 1974).

Therapies with an element of action

Alexander technique is a system of mind-body re-education which fosters a new way of looking at and 'using' the self.

Autogenics is a method of mind-over-body control based on a specific discipline for relaxing parts of the body by means of autosuggestion.

Behaviour therapy acts to modify an individual's behaviour through a process of learning. Methods include systematic desensitization (the individual learns to relax in situations that previously produced anxiety), assertiveness training, reinforcement of adaptive behaviours and extinction of maladaptive ones, modelling of appropriate behaviour and techniques for self-regulation.

Cognitive behaviour therapy uses behaviour modification techniques and also incorporates procedures for changing maladaptive beliefs. The therapist helps the individual to replace irrational interpretations of events with more realistic ones.

Dance therapy uses dance and movement to promote emotional well-being, fitness and good posture.

Dramatherapy, developed by Sue Jennings, is based on theatre art and is a way of understanding more about ourselves and the world. Through the 'dramatic' distancing of the self (through theatre art we put a distance between self and the character) clients come closer to the issues that need to be experienced. Paradoxically, in Dramatherapy, distancing brings us closer.

Feldenkrais technique aims to help a person to recognize and correct bad habits of body use. This is done through awareness and exercise.

Gestalt therapy, developed by Fritz Perls, aims to help people become aware of their 'whole' personality by working through unresolved conflicts and uncovering blocks. Therapists work with one individual at a time.

Gravity guidance works on the premise that many of the body's strains are caused by the downward pull of gravity. Practitioners aim to use this force to reverse the negative strains. The main way of doing this is simply by hanging upside down.

Group therapy provides an opportunity for individuals to explore their own attitudes and behaviour and the attitudes and behaviour of others. Group therapy can take many forms and is used by therapists of various orientations. Sessions can be held anywhere (hospitals, community spaces, school halls).

Hug therapy involves people being open to the child within them who needs love, safety, support, caring and play, and reaching out to the same needs in others.

Hydrotherapy involves the therapeutic use of water, taken either internally or externally, including the use of hot and cold baths, Turkish baths and saunas.

Meditation, as practised by the eastern religions, is used in the west to improve health and physical and mental relaxation, or as a psychotherapy.

Naturotherapy is a group of related natural-health disciplines used to promote health and to show people how they can alter their lifestyles so as to avoid future illness. The systems involved include hydrotherapy, diet therapy and relaxation techniques.

Neuro Linguistic Programming (NLP), developed by Bandler and Grindler in the early 1970s, put forward that we can alter (or reprogramme) our behaviour and memories to make our lives happier (liveable). Through a process of 'kinesthetics', clients are encouraged to discover the meaning of 'words': our personal history. Words are subjective, and each word will have a slightly different meaning or sensation for different people. The meanings we give will depend on our experiences, and our experiences are our history.

Psychodrama, developed by Moreno (from his theatre of spontaneity), provides a new frame of reference. Through psychodrama deeper changes can take place and can have a cathartic effect on the participants. People are often confused about the difference between psychodrama and dramatherapy. One major difference is that psychodrama is very much to do with the closeness of one's 'own life', while dramatherapy establishes the 'dramatic distance' through creating a story.

'The Renaissance Magus, Paracelsus, warned that the guru [therapist] should avoid simply revealing "the naked truth". He should use images, allegories, figures, wondrous speech, or other hidden, roundabout ways' (Sheldon Kopp, *If You Meet the Buddha on the Road, Kill Him!*, Sheldon Press, London, 1974).

EVALUATION

Evaluating your work

When working with any group it is important not only to continually assess how people feel participating within the group, but also to let them evaluate the whole. This is important for them, being able to write down how they feel, but it is also important for the group leader because it helps to identify what worked and what did not. Evaluation helps to keep a tab on progress and helps in the direction. It also offers some kind of a guide for outsiders to see how a particular group session went. *It does not take long to evaluate — and it really is worth doing.*

Evaluate at the end of a session or at the end of a run of sessions with the same group. Hand out the evaluation sheets and get people to fill them in and hand them back to you *before they go*: if you let people take them home to fill in and return to you, not only will people forget some of the workshop, but you will probably find that over half the participants will not remember to return the evaluation sheet.

The following is a sample evaluation sheet which you may photocopy (I would recommend enlarging it to A4 and double-siding, if possible) or use as a base for one of your own.

Workshop evaluation

Please spend 10 minutes filling in this sheet. We need this feedback to ensure that your needs are met and to improve future workshops.

Name (optional)	Date
Address (optional)	
Please state in what capacity you attended	
School/group name	
Type of workshop	
Your overall impression of the workshop was (please tick) ☐ Excellent ☐ Good ☐ Fair ☐ Poor	
The practical value of the workshop was (please tick) ☐ Excellent ☐ Good ☐ Fair ☐ Poor	
What was the most successful feature of the workshop?	
What was the least successful feature of the workshop?	

© A Hickson, 1995. This evaluation sheet may be photocopied for administrative use only.

If you could change one thing about the workshop, what would it be?
Do you think that more or less time should have been spent on any section?
Were there any areas which you wanted to find out about that were not included in the workshop?
Please comment on the tutor(s)' effectiveness and presentation
Overall, did this workshop reach your expectations? Yes/No. If not, can you say why?
Will anything you have learned from this workshop be of practical use to you in your life/work/studies? How?

© A Hickson, 1995. This evaluation sheet may be photocopied for administrative use only.

BIBLIOGRAPHY

Atkinson RL, Atkinson RC, Smith EE & Hilgard ER, *Introduction to Psychology*, Harcourt, London, 1985.
Bandler R & Grinder J, *Frogs into Princes*, Eden Grove, Utah, 1979.
Barker C, *Theatre Games*, Methuen, London, 1977.
Berger J, *Ways of Seeing*, Penguin, London, 1972.
Berne E, *Games People Play*, Penguin, Harmondsworth, 1964.
Boal A, *Theatre of the Oppressed*, Pluto Press, New York, 1988.
Boal A, *Games for Actors and Non-Actors*, Routledge, London, 1992.
Brandes D & Phillips H, *Gamesters' Handbook*, Stanley Thornes, Cheltenham, 1977.
Brook P, *The Empty Space*, Penguin, London, 1972.
Cattanach A, *Drama for People with Special Needs*, A & C Black, London, 1992.
Christen L, *Drama Skills for Life*, Currency Press, Sydney, 1992.
Coppet de D, *Understanding Rituals*, Routledge, London, 1992.
Cox J (ed), *Transcultural Psychiatry*, Croom Helm, London, 1986.
Dayton T, *Drama Games*, Innerlook Inc, Florida, 1990.
Dynes R, *Creative Games in Groupwork*, Winslow Press, Bicester, 1990.
Foster R, *Knowing my Bones*, A & C Black, London, 1976.
Fox J (ed), *The Essential Moreno*, Springer, New York, 1987.
Grotowski J, *Towards a Poor Theatre*, Methuen, London, 1969.
Hewitt J, *Meditation*, Hodder & Stoughton, London, 1978.
Hickson A, *Workshop Teachers Pack*, Hey! Hey! Theatre Co Ltd, London, 1991.
Jennings S, *Remedial Drama*, A & C Black, London, 1978.
Jennings S, *Dramatherapy with Families, Groups and Individuals*, Jessica Kingsley, London, 1987.
Jennings S, *Dramatherapy Theory and Practice*, Vol. 1, Routledge, London, 1987.
Jennings S, *Dramatherapy Theory and Practice*, Vol. 2, Routledge, London, 1992.
Jennings S, Cattanach A, Mitchell S, Chesner A & Meldrum B, *The Handbook of Dramatherapy*, Routledge, London, 1994.
Johnstone K, *Impro*, Methuen, London, 1979.

Keating K, *The Little Book of Hugs,* Angus, London, 1983.
Kirsta A, *Stress Survival,* Gala, London, 1989.
Kopp S, *If You Meet the Buddha on the Road, Kill Him!,* Sheldon Press, London, 1974.
Kumiega J, *The Theatre of Grotowski,* Methuen, London, 1985.
Littlewood R & Lipsedge M, *Aliens and Alienists,* Penguin, London, 1982.
McCallion M, *The Voice Book,* Faber & Faber, London, 1988.
Midgley M, *Beast & Man,* Methuen, London, 1978.
Moreno JL, Moreno ZT & Hole AN, *Group Psychotherapy and Psychodrama,* vol. XXVII, nos 1—4, Beacon House, New York, 1974.
Murphy RC, *Psychotherapy Based on Human Longing,* Pendle Hill Leaflets, London, 1960.
Spolin V, *Theatre Games for Rehearsal,* Northwestern University Press, Evanston, 1985.
Weber A, *Introduction to Psychology,* Harper Collins, London, 1991.
Winnicott DW, *Playing and Reality,* Pelican, London, 1974.

ALPHABETICAL LIST OF ACTIVITIES

Animals, 59

Back to self, 106
Basic sculpt, 144
Blind catch, 87
Blind face, 112
Blind return, 88
Blind slalom, 91
Blind sound, 85
Breath support and control, 45
British bulldog, 23

C

Carnival time, 113
Catch my name, 98
Change the image, 142
Change the image of the
    object, 153
Change the president, 116
Counting sound, 83

Deflate me, 80

Excalibur, 128
Explosion tig, 130

F

Face masks, 62
Feel the object, 92
Fill that space, 102
Flying to the moon, 122
Follow the palm, 119
Forum theatre 1, 159
Forum theatre 2, 161
Forum theatre model, 156

Goalkeeper, 90
Group body sculpt, 146
Group hum, 81

Hat and run, 93
Heaven and hell, 30
Hello, 140
Hot seat 1, 114
Hot seat 2, 115
How many As in one A?, 123
How yer doin'?, 103

Image of the family, 176
Image of the group, 149
Image of the object, 152
Interpreter, 84
It's not my party, 131

Leapfrog, 21
Loosening up physically, 43

Massage circle, 107
Minimum surface contact, 109
Mirror, mirror on the wall, 66
Modelling, 55
Moving group hum, 82
Muscles, 108
My family, 148

Object balance, 111

Paper dance, 22
Pass the clap, 137
Per to per, 117
Policeman, 132

Races 1, 31
Races 2, 32
Races 3, 33
Races 4, 34
Races 5, 35
Races 6, 36
Races 7, 37
Races 8, 38
Races 9, 39
Races 10, 40
Recap, 105
Revelations, 168
Rhythm shoes, 74
Ritual 1, 171
Ritual 2, 172
Ritual 3, 173
Ritual 4, 174
Role reversal, 170

Salt and pepper, 99
Save me, 136
Shakespeare 1, 163
Shakespeare 2, 164
Shakespeare 3, 165
Silence is golden, 133
Slow-motion race, 110
Sound and rhythm of the circle, 77
Sound of the circle, 76
Speech and articulation, 48
Sticky paper, 134

T

Ten questions, 154
Thai-boxing match, 24
The bag, 175
The blind car, 124
The crawl 1, 25
The crawl 2, 26
The crawl 3, 27
The crawl 4, 28
The crawl 5, 29
The cross and the circle, 101
The embassy ball, 138
The game of machines, 135
The game of power, 120
The Institute of Silly Walks, 58
The magnet, 89
The vampire of Strasbourg, 125
This is my house, 68
Tip-to-top, 19
Tone and resonance, 46
Tongue-twisters, 50
Transforming oppression, 147
Twin mirrors, 127

U

Using Shakespeare, 166

V

Variety and colour, 49
Visualize the sound 1, 78
Visualize the sound 2, 79
Volleyball, 151

W

Walking millipede, 118
What's in a bottle?, 97
What was I doing?, 104
Which word witch?, 129
Who am I?, 72
Who is the leader?, 71
Who is the mirror?, 70
Who said 'Arghh'?, 86
Wink murder, 64

197

The Creative Activity Series ...

This unique series common theme is to provide creative activity ideas for use with groups of all ages.

Creative Action Methods in Groupwork
Andy Hickson
Highly practical and accessible, with emphasis on participative groupwork and good working practices, this unique manual outlines action method techniques for exploring difficulties and problems.

Creative Writing in Groupwork
Robin Dynes
Here are over 100 stimulating activities designed to help participants express themselves, explore situations, compare ideas and develop both imagination and creative ability.

Creative Games in Groupwork
Robin Dynes
Presented in a format that immediately allows you to see what materials are needed, how much preparation is required and how each game is played, this practical book will be of real value to the user.

Creative Movement & Dance in Groupwork
Helen Payne
This innovative book explores the link between movement and emotion and provides 180 activities and ideas with a clear rationale for the use of dance movement to enrich therapy and programmes.

Creative Drama in Groupwork
Sue Jennings
150 ideas for drama in this completely practical manual make it a veritable treasure trove which will inspire everyone to run drama sessions creatively, enjoyably and effectively.

Creative Art in Groupwork
Jean Campbell
Highly accessible, this manual contains 142 art activities developed specifically for use with groups of people of all ages.

Creative Relaxation in Groupwork
Irene Tubbs
With more than 100 activities, this book discusses the benefits of relaxation, covers theoretical and practical relaxation methods, provides constructive guidelines for good practice and incorporates actual workshop themes.

For further information or to obtain a free copy of the Speechmark catalogue, please contact:

Telford Road • Bicester
Oxon OX26 4LQ • UK

Tel: 01869 244644
Fax: 01869 320040
www.speechmark.net